EXECUTIVE RETIREMENT MANAGEMENT

EXECUTIVE RETIREMENT MANAGEMENT

A Manager's Guide to the Planning and Implementation of a Successful Retirement

Jack J. Leedy, M.D.

and

James Wynbrandt

Facts On File Publications
New York, New York ● Oxford, England

EXECUTIVE RETIREMENT MANAGEMENT

Grateful acknowledgment is given for the use of material on p. 107 adapted by permission of the publisher, from *The Retirement Decision: How American Managers View Their Prospects*, an AMA Survey Report, by Robert Jud, p.21, © 1981 AMACOM, a division of American Management Association, New York. All rights reserved.

Library of Congress Cataloging-in-Publication Data

Leedy, Jack J., 1921-
    Executive retirement management.

    Bibliography: p.
    Includes index.
    1. Executives—United States—Retirement—Management.
    2. Retirement—United States—Management. I. Wynbrandt, James. II. Title.
    HD7125.L43 1987   658.4′07132   86-24010
    ISBN 0-8160-1286-5

Printed in the United States of America
10 9 8 7 6 5 4 3 2 1

Interior design by Debbie Glasserman
Composition by Facts On File/Maxwell Photographics

2313122

CONTENTS

ACKNOWLEDGMENTS

We'd like to thank the following people and organizations who were so helpful to us in writing this book:

Henry Wallfesh and John N. Migliaccio of Retirement Advisors, Inc.; Dr. Robert Butler of the Mount Sinai Medical Center; Carol Cronin of the Washington Business Group on Health; Clare Corbett and David Carboni of the International Society of Preretirement Planners; Barbara Katzman of the National Institute on Aging; Jan Davidson and Cathy Ventrell-Monsees of the American Association of Retired Persons; David Gray of the National Executive Service Corps; Dr. Harry Evarts of the American Management Associations; the staff of ProMedia for research assistance; Joseph S. Perkins of Polaroid; Carol Bartley of Heidrick and Struggles, Inc.; Richard Lannamann of Russell Reynolds Associates, Inc.; Gary Wyatt and Joan L. Finn of KMG Main Hurdman; James Davis of System Development Corporation; Arthur A. Pumo of IBM; Joseph K. Sapora of Hay/Huggins Company, Inc.; Dr. S. J. Schieber of the Wyatt Company; Harold B. Mers of the Forty Plus Club of New York; Eugene Daly; Maxine Wineapple; Leonard J. Lamm of the New School for Social Research; and Victoria Starr.

Special thanks to Bob Markel, Kate Kelly and Ed Knappman for their encouragement and support for this project.

PREFACE

The institution of retirement is changing. Retirees are changing. Society is changing. Nowhere has the confluence of these currents had more impact than among today's maturing managers. They are approaching the future with a greater concentration of health, wealth and wisdom than any maturing population in the history of the world.

At the turn of the century, the average retirement for an American male lasted less than five years. Today, with the life expectancy of a 65-year-old hovering around 80, and the trend toward early retirement accelerating, it's not uncommon for almost one-third of one's life to be spent in retirement. This dramatically increased time is only exceeded by the new opportunities maturing executives can take advantage of—if they plan and prepare. Yet having a positive attitude about retirement isn't enough to ensure success, as was made clear in one of the seminal articles on retirement management, written by Leland Bradford, former head of the National Training Laboratories, and published in the Harvard Business Review of November-December 1979.

"After 25 years of working under the strain of building an organization . . . I was ready for the beautiful promised land of retirement. I persuaded my wife to leave our lovely Georgetown home and move to North Carolina, where I could golf to my heart's content and enjoy relief from the stress of having to make daily decisions. I thought it would be just wonderful."

"How wrong I was! The first year was awful. The organization

P A R T I

EXECUTIVES AND RETIREMENT: THE CAREER CONNECTION

John C. Bowen was a dynamic and aggressive executive. He could make a boardroom shake, a division snap to attention. He helped turn an aging Midwestern auto parts supplier into a thriving, national, diversified manufacturing company.

At 49 Bowen was named CEO. At 56 he added chairman to the title. At 62 came mandatory retirement. Seven months later came a heart attack that almost ended his life.

John C. Bowen's story is all too typical of executives in organizations large and small across the country: managers who are successful in their careers, but unprepared for the challenges of retirement. If you're a maturing executive, you could be one of them. What can you do about it? *Stop thinking about your career, and start thinking about your future!*

The dangers facing today's retiring managers are real. Statistics and anecdotes paint a frightening picture of heart attacks, strokes, hypertension, alcohol abuse and other health problems among retired executives. And there are problems the statistics don't reveal—emotional turmoil, domestic problems, depression, an inability to find meaning in a life without career.

These aren't scare tactics. They're facts, a realistic catalog of the problems many executives encounter in retirement. But for every John C. Bowen, there's a success story of an executive who's seized the growing array of options and opportunities and turned retirement into the most rewarding and dynamic chapter of his life. A maturing electronics entrepreneur sells his company to make a solo sailing expedition around the world. An auto executive fulfills a lifelong dream of becoming a college professor. A former manager starts a multimillion-dollar consulting business. And a retired actor moves into politics and eventually captures the highest office in the land.

2

Thousands of former executives are enjoying retirements that are less ambitious, but no less successful. There are second careers, expanded leisure opportunities, financial freedom. It's all there for the taking for those who have realistic attitudes about the future, and take the time to plan for it. Retirement can be either heaven or hell, and there's only one thing separating the two—you!

Managers and Management Careers

Executives aren't the only people who face retirement. Why do they need to follow a specialized approach to planning? There are three compelling reasons:

1. *Career Relationship.* Executives have a unique relationship with their careers, making them more emotionally connected to their occupations than hourly wage earners and lower-level salaried employees. Surveys consistently show that managers rate their own work as more satisfying than hourly workers rate theirs. Additionally, executives exhibit strong proactive personalities that find a positive outlet in their careers. Career relationship must be recognized and often compensated for in order to create a successful retirement.

2. *The Revamping of Retirement.* Massive changes in the corporation and in society profoundly affect the manager's retirement options and opportunities. The new picture includes second careers, early retirement, alteration of mandatory retirement policies, corporate upheaval, demographic shifts, improved health, and the public's more favorable perception of the mature individual. These changes demand a new approach to retirement planning and retirement.

3. *Management Skills.* The management skills executives have developed during their careers can be applied to retirement. Taking advantage of this know-how and professional commitment significantly increases the chance of post-career success. Yet the challenges of retirement are different from those of career, and executives need to know how to apply their management skills to achieving post-career goals.

Later on we'll go into detail about the tremendous changes the institution of retirement is undergoing, and how to use your management skills to capitalize on them. First, let's look at the executive's career relationship.

CHAPTER ONE

CAREER RELATIONSHIP AND THE RETIREMENT TRANSITION

Successful executives have a high degree of career commitment, career identification and career satisfaction. Together, these qualities form a direct link connecting the executive's career to his emotional well-being.

Career Commitment
Top managers are tremendously dedicated to their careers, mentally and physically. Long after the factory floor has emptied, the manager is often still in his office. While other salaried personnel relax over the weekend, he may be preparing strategy for an upcoming contract negotiation, or pouring over quarterly reviews. A recent survey of senior executives found more than 43% reported working between 60 and 69 hours a week. More than 42% reported working from 50 to 60 hours a week, while under 5% reported working less than 50 hours a week. Professionals (doctors, lawyers, architects, etc.) exhibit similar dedication.

5

This commitment can reach unhealthy levels, or arise from unhealthy motives (as we'll see later), but it's a common denominator among managers, and a powerful force that has to be reckoned with in retirement.

Career Identification

Managers often see their work as an extension of themselves: the "I am my career" syndrome. The less structured nature of management positions gives them more opportunity to put their personality, their individual "stamp," on projects and procedures. This personalization reinforces career identification. Some executives may admit to feeling they were "born" to occupy certain management positions.

Company training, corporate culture and shared workplace goals further add to this career-oriented definition of self. Constant association with other professionals bolsters this identification.

Career Satisfaction

The executive's work is tough and demanding, but the challenges and perks of executive life make it highly satisfying. There's a high degree of control over environment, rich financial rewards, and feelings of power and responsibility. The success-oriented personality finds a perfect outlet in the struggle to attain well-defined goals and symbols of achievement. The resultant career satisfaction binds the manager to his career.

Looking over these three positive career components, it's easy to see why many executives don't want to retire. But this doesn't tell the whole story of why so many executives do such a poor job of preparing for their post-career life.

So how can a top executive who charts a future of growth and profitability for his company in an uncertain and treacherous business environment show a lack of foresight in planning for his own future? In a nutshell, it's because the emotional issues surrounding retirement can be extremely troubling, and thus set a strong denial mechanism in motion. This can be true for any prospective retiree, but for executives, with their positive career relationship, the denial mechanism is especially powerful.

Retirement isn't only the end of a career. It's a time of severing professional and social relationships, of coming to terms with aging and mortality, of dealing with a tremendous feeling of loss of control and uncertainty about the future. The way you think about yourself changes. Your relationship with your family and community changes. It's stressful and anxiety provoking. Indeed, according to the Social Readjustment Rating Scale, developed by T. H. Holmes and R. H. Rahe, retirement is in the Top 10 of life's most stress-producing events. No wonder many executives prefer to play ostrich when it comes to planning for the future. But facing retirement doesn't have to be as traumatic and difficult as most executives make it.

The Four Stages of Retirement Transition

Retirement would be a lot easier to manage if executives used a better model for visualizing it. Most see retirement as a singular event—the day they stop coming to work. Everything before is career, everything after is retirement. With this "event-oriented" view, retirement seems like a brick wall appearing out of the fog on a fast-moving freeway. A disruptive and destructive collision takes place.

But a successful retirement starts long before the final day at the office or the last toast at a testimonial dinner. It's an orderly and planned transition that provides the right framework for working through the emotional turmoil that approaching retirement triggers. Let's get back on the freeway for a minute. The retirement transition is a gradual deceleration. You're not slowing down in the physical sense, you're shifting emotional gears from career priorities to personal priorities. The transition carries you from the career fast lane onto the ramp to your future. Planning and executing the right transition will keep you in positive control of your future, alert you to the possibilities ahead, and help you avoid the pitfalls and potholes that keep many former executives from getting their post-career lives in gear.

A successful retirement starts with a four-stage transition. It's important to understand the function and goal of each:

1. Realization
2. Acceptance
3. Disengagement
4. Separation

REALIZATION

Realization means understanding you will retire; this is a concrete, not an abstract, understanding. It's the one stage shared by all retirees; but too many executives avoid understanding until it's too late to do anything about it. Realization should begin five to ten years before retirement. The wrong approach is exemplified by the first Realization experience of one former corporate executive.

"About six weeks before I was set to retire my staff took me out for drinks. They called it a 'beginning of the end' party. I was on my second scotch when it hit me, I mean really hit me for the first time—I was retiring!"

The key to healthy Realization is to begin thinking about retirement well in advance of your retirement date. In the office environment it means assessing your career and your future honestly. At home it means talking about the future with your spouse and other family members. (In Part III you'll find exercises for the office and home that will help you work through each stage of your retirement transition.) A successful Realization will trigger two reactions:

- Emotional
- Pragmatic

Once these reactions are aroused, you will feel compelled to address them. This signals the next stage of the transition. (See Part III.)

ACCEPTANCE

Acceptance is the process of dealing with and resolving the emotional and pragmatic reactions triggered by Realization. During Acceptance you'll come to terms with what your career means to you, and start thinking about and planning for life without it. Involvement and support from spouse and other family members will become increasingly important during this stage.

Once you "realize" you're going to retire, you may find yourself confronting a host of negative emotions (more about them in a moment). These feelings can be very disturbing, and once they begin surfacing it's important to avoid the temptation to rebury them.

Draw them out, confront them and conquer them. Don't expect to resolve all these conflicts overnight. Some of the more troubling issues may follow you into retirement.

The negative emotional reaction will be offset by a pragmatic one. The reality of retirement is a powerful inducement to get you planning for it. Making your plans concrete helps you cope with the emotional turmoil of Acceptance. You'll feel much more positive and in control of your post-career future if you start taking steps now to direct it.

The pitfalls of improper Acceptance are summed up by the former national sales manager of a retail chain: "It was six months after I left, and I still couldn't believe I'd retired. I kept thinking I'd go back in a few days. It was like a vacation that went on way too long . . . I kept waiting to go back to work."

An inability to successfully resolve these emotions and begin making realistic plans for the future will keep you mired in the past. Executives who can't "accept" retirement thrust themselves into a situation they're unable to reverse and unable to reconcile. For them, the future is bitter and isolated. (See Part III.)

DISENGAGEMENT

In the office, Realization and Acceptance are essentially mental exercises. They get you mentally prepared for the future while you are still fully involved with your career. Disengagement introduces an action-oriented approach to the retirement transition. During this stage there's a reduction of emotional involvement with your career and a selective reduction of actual management involvement. As we'll discuss later, this stage is vitally important both for you and the company you're leaving. On the home front, you will step up the testing of plans for your post-career lifestyle and activities. You will continue to involve your spouse and family in planning and decisions, at least to the extent they'll be affected. You will increase involvement with post-career social and organizational networks.

Disengagement should begin between two and five years before retirement. The active steps you take during this stage will help you deal with lingering issues of Acceptance. Even when the first two transitional stages have been neglected until late in a career, a comprehensive Disengagement agenda can overcome a slow start in retirement planning, as the following recollection of a retired senior vice president of an electrical manufacturing company shows.

"When I was sixty I didn't have a clue about what I'd do with myself when I retired, I was so wrapped up in work. I made a conscious effort to step back and make plans for after retirement. I delegated more responsibility, took more vacation time, investigated other business opportunities, and by the time I retired I was totally prepared."

A successful Disengagement weans you from emotional dependence on your present career, and paves the way for a smooth entrance into retirement. Even if you plan to keep working in retirement, Disengagement is necessary to sever the connections to your career and those thoughts of missed opportunities and unfinished business. It puts a cap on your career, leaving you free to move onto the next chapter of your life. (See Part III.)

SEPARATION

The first three retirement transition stages take you out of your career and prepare you for retirement. Separation begins after you retire, and marks the start of a healthy and rewarding post-career lifestyle. It starts directly after the whirlwind of activity that usually accompanies retirement (an immediate post-career vacation, the last post-career retirement party) is over. Final career-related issues are resolved and gradually replaced by concerns about achieving post-career goals. You'll fine-tune the plans you made before retirement and aggressively put them into practice. Relocation, a second career and serious involvement in volunteer or other activities are undertaken. Careful attention is paid to retirement adaptation to make sure the direction you set off in isn't a knee-jerk reaction to the severance of career ties. You'll become comfortable knowing your career is a completed chapter of your life. And you'll be busy writing the next one.

"I had plenty of plans for what I'd do in retirement, but after I retired I just couldn't find the energy to do anything. I don't think I missed my job that much, I'd pretty much come to terms with the fact I'd be retiring. But the more difficulty I had motivating myself, the more depressed I got."

As this public relations executive's experiences indicate, a retirement transition that gets you out of your career can still fail you in retirement if you don't follow through with Separation. (See Part VI.)

TRANSITIONAL STAGE OVERLAP

The transitional stages of retirement don't exist in isolation. They often overlap, and issues you felt were resolved in one stage may appear again much later. For example, during Disengagement, you may wake up one morning and have trouble believing you're actually going to retire (which was presumably dealt with in Realization). Or during Separation, after you've retired, it may strike you as grossly unfair that you were subject to mandatory retirement (an Acceptance issue). However, as long as you concentrate on going through these stages one at a time, you'll be following an excellent roadmap for minimizing emotional problems and maximizing satisfaction in retirement.

The Negative Emotions of the Retirement Transition

We've talked about the potentially rocky road to retirement success. Now let's get specific about the troubling emotions you may face. The stresses they create make the importance of a well-planned retirement transition obvious.

Each executive responds to retirement differently; and not all react negatively to it. But all of those who do react negatively, often even those looking forward to retirement, will experience some combination of the same emotions. Four negative emotions encompass the variety of troubling feelings you may encounter:

1. Fear
2. Anger
3. Rejection
4. Grief

FEAR

Any change provokes stress and anxiety, even changes for the better, such as marriage or coming into a large sum of money. We've already mentioned that retirement ranks high in the catalog of stress-producing events. The stress and anxiety retirement may provoke can reach the level of fear.

Fear of the Unknown

A career has a reassuring degree of structure. Retirement raises questions of what lies ahead, of your ability to meet the challenges. As one maturing executive put it, "I've always been successful, but that was as part of a management team. I don't know if I can make it on my own."

Fear of Loss of Identity

Having defined yourself through your career, you may subconsciously feel you will cease to exist once you retire. You will be "no one," stripped of the role you've spent years playing. You fear becoming transparent.

Fear of Loss of Control

Executives receive instant and positive reinforcement about their ability to influence their environments. Retirement doesn't provide this feedback, and the subliminal message of impotency inherent in this loss of control can be terrifying. The power you've been able to use to exercise your control is instantly gone. The plug's been pulled.

Financial Fears

Even the most financially secure retired executive is prone to worries about money. Over the course of a career you've come to equate work with pay. This leads to subconscious thoughts that without work, there won't be money, and so creates crippling attitudes about personal finances.

Fear of Aging and Mortality

Retirement sends a strong message that you're getting older. There's a tendency to feel the best is behind you, to become morose and despondent. You may view yourself as washed up, through. In the extreme, this fear can become a self-fulfilling prophecy. Some shut themselves off from life, "waiting for the end," instead of taking effective control of their post-career lives.

Fear has the ability to immobilize, or to make you dart about in terrifying confusion. Fear tends to occupy the mind to the exclusion of other emotions, certainly those of pleasure and optimism. Allowing fear to prevail negates the possibility of addressing the future with a confident and balanced attitude.

ANGER

Anger is a standard response to retirement. You needn't face compulsory retirement to feel angry about leaving work. Anger is the displacement of the frustration and resentment you may feel. It can take many forms and be pointed in just as many directions.

Anger at the Organization
An obvious place for you to direct your anger at is your company. You may feel "forced out," "kicked aside" or upset that more efforts weren't made to prepare you for this change.

Anger at Oneself
Executives undergoing retirement difficulties may blame themselves for not doing more to prepare. This anger exhibits itself most strongly after retirement, when lack of planning begins to make itself evident. Some may even "blame" themselves for growing older and having to retire.

The more hectic the pre-retirement work environment, and the less preparation undertaken, the higher the levels of these two kinds of anger. The former director of marketing at a domestic textile company felt a great deal of anger at his company and at himself for his post-retirement troubles. The company had been taking a beating from imported fabrics, and running hard just to stay even. Neither the organization nor the executive had taken the time to prepare for retirement.

Anger at Others
Feelings that co-workers or family don't appreciate the change you are undergoing can trigger irrational bursts of anger. Even if others don't do anything to provoke it, general unhappiness and dis-

satisfaction with the prospect of retirement can emerge as anger, directed at those closest to you.

Anger at Specific Individuals

Rivals, real or imagined, subordinates and superiors who you haven't always seen eye-to-eye with, may become lightening rods for anger. Quarrels may be precipitated in final attempts at situational dominance.

Displaced Anger

Anger is often directed at inanimate objects. You may become short-tempered, easily riled. Small frustrations you would have easily handled in the past suddenly make you fume, and become major preoccupations.

Ultimately, anger diverts you from paying attention to post-career planning, and perhaps worse, can interfere with sound decision-making.

REJECTION

Feelings of being unwanted, unneeded and unloved can be part of the retirement picture. A company's attempt to assist the executive's retirement may even be seen through the lens of rejection.

"I knew they wanted to get rid of me. The last year they had three hot shots gunning for my job, and they made me sit around doing nothing. After all I did for them, they just squeezed me out. I was already out the door by the time I retired."

The interesting thing about this executive is that he was responding to his company's rather progressive retirement program, aimed at providing a continuity of management and retirement training.

Professional Rejection

Executives who feel victimized by retirement may look for signs that people are glad to see them go. You may see rejection in procedural changes counter to the way you ran things, or in suggestions or ideas of yours that aren't adopted. You may retreat into a "kick me while I'm down" mode of thinking, and succeed in turning your suspicion of rejection into a self-fulfilling prophecy.

Personal Rejection

The executive who feels unwanted and unneeded at the office as retirement approaches looks for similar signals in his personal life.

Retirement can be a time of extreme emotional vulnerability, and you may take grim satisfaction in proving it will be every bit as bad as you thought it would be. You're on the lookout for any treatment that can reinforce your feelings of rejection.

Internal Rejection

Feelings of external rejection are often projections of ambivalence about your future role. Used to being the "executive," the "breadwinner," or identifying yourself in some other career-oriented capacity, you may subconsciously reject yourself once you no longer fill the position.

Those who look for rejection are often looking for signals to confirm subconscious feelings about themselves. Times of emotional vulnerability are when you are most prone to these feelings, like a weakened body falling prey to the flu. Rejection, like fear, can be a paralyzing emotion, but it operates in a different way. Rather than making you feel threatened from the outside, it makes you feel worthless inside. And once you feel worthless, there's no reason to bother trying to improve your situation.

GRIEF

Grief, along with anger at oneself, is most pronounced during the latter stages of Disengagement and during Separation, once your career is over. It's not an easily compartmentalized emotion. As you take stock of your career and your life, many aspects will be tinged with grief. Even memories of the good times may seem sad knowing they can never be recaptured.

For all the promise of retirement, no one can deny that it's also a time of letting go, of leaving behind things that have had great meaning and personal importance for decades—friendships that are severed or drastically altered, dreams of career possibilities to be relinquished, triumphs never to be repeated. Saying goodbye to this creates grief, a feeling of loss or disconnectedness, of mourning.

Grief is a normal and healthy reaction to retirement, and you should give yourself a chance to experience it. It leads to a catharsis that helps you resolve your feelings about your career, and allows you to move freely into the future. The danger is in covering up grief, not letting yourself resolve your feelings. This can keep you from successfully separating from your career.

As you go through your retirement transition, be ready to deal with these negative emotions. They'll most likely appear, since they are a normal part of retirement. Your goal is to work through them, not wallow in them.

Feeling angry, fearful, grief-stricken or rejected doesn't mean you have an emotional problem. These feelings are natural responses to the disturbing issues of retirement, and need to be experienced to be resolved. The real problems start when these emotions aren't properly managed, are ignored or underestimated. When this happens, we begin to see mental and physical health problems arise. The deterioration can be startlingly quick.

On the mental health side, the most common result is depression. This is usually the first sign that an executive is having problems facing or managing retirement. It can begin well before retirement, if an executive can't deal with the issues usually resolved during Acceptance. The key to avoiding depression, or any serious retirement-related mental health problem, is effective emotional management in the retirement transition.

Physical health is tied equally to emotional management. The majority of major health problems within the last five years of career and first five years of retirement are stress-related. And the stresses that precipitate these problems are often the result of retirement-related emotional difficulties.

If we can control the emotional upheaval of retirement, we can control the heart attacks, strokes, the stress-related diseases that threaten so many retiring executives.

CHAPTER TWO

MANAGEMENT PERSONALITIES IN RETIREMENT

So far we've discussed three common denominators among executives facing retirement:

1. A strong career relationship
2. A need for transitional planning
3. A set of negative emotions to contend with

This is where the similarity ends. No two executives are alike, and therefore transition and retIrement strategies have to be tailored individually. The clues for designing the right strategy are found in management style. Here, the questions of major interest are how and why an executive has achieved success. And at the heart of this question is the reason why managers who have triumphed in their careers can fail miserably in retirement. *What's good for the organization isn't always good for the individual.*

In other words, the traits that breed corporate success can also assure retirement failure. We're not suggesting that career success and retirement failure go hand in hand. All other things being equal, the more successful executive has a better chance at retirement success because he possesses a better set of management skills that can be applied to retirement. What we use to compare successful executives in their chances for retirement success are the motivations that propelled them to the top in business.

Among formerly successful executives who've encountered serious adjustment problems in retirement, there are four management personalities most prone to post-career difficulties. Even well-adjusted executives can possess characteristics of one or more of these personalities; knowing if you exhibit any of these traits will help you look out for the problems associated with each of them. An executive who demonstrates extremes of behavior in any one of these management personality types must be cognizant of the potential adjustment difficulties ahead, and be prepared to adopt an aggressive strategy to deal with them.

These are the four problematic management personalities:

1. The Reactive Manager
2. The Company Man
3. The Overachiever
4. The Combat Vet

There are transition strategies for the office and home environments for each personality type, and strategies to overcome post-career adjustment problems as well. Right now we'll introduce you to each of these personality types, and to an executive who strongly exhibited characteristics of each behavior in his career.

The Reactive Manager

The Reactive Manager is stress driven. He needs excitement and operates an environment guaranteed to generate it. His style of management is among the things they don't teach you at Harvard Business School.

He likes to manage by instinct, dealing with things "as they come up," and is often not a good planner. This assures that the Reactive

Manager and his team will always be turning around to face flames. He loves fighting fires and crisis management. When his gambles pay off, the Reactive Manager may be described as "bold" and "innovative."

In larger organizations, the Reactive Manager usually has not been promoted from within, having earned a reputation elsewhere of being aggressive and driven, though sometimes unorthodox. He commands fierce loyalty, though he may be hard to work with. He may exhibit entrepreneurial tendencies.

Some will create crises in order to maintain the level of excitement and stress they crave. Among their typical ploys: ordering constant reorganizations or shake-ups, putting off decisions, changing their minds, leaving tasks unfinished until the last minute, or habitually setting unachievable goals.

JOHN C. BOWEN

After graduating with a degree in engineering, John C. Bowen began working for various small manufacturing companies as a designer/troubleshooter. His knowledge of engineering and hands-on style were rewarded with higher salary and more responsibility by a succession of employers, as he gradually shifted from technical to management positions.

"I moved around a lot in the beginning of my career. I needed new challenges all the time. I got uncomfortable if things were running too smoothly."

At the age of 35, Bowen was hired by American Industries to help with the operations of Wrightcraft, a privately held automotive parts company A.I. had bought some 18 months before.

"Right after they bought Wrightcraft they landed some good-sized government contracts, but they were having trouble filling the orders. One plant was really giving them problems. They couldn't get the new machine tools on line, there were problems training people, everything was a mess. The guy I replaced had lasted, oh, maybe four months before he threw in the towel . . . I'd developed a reputation in certain manufacturing circles for getting things done. I guess that's why they asked me aboard."

Bowen was sent in to get things moving at the Terre Haute plant.

"I didn't want to spend time developing flow charts or conducting studies. I acted. I was looking for results, and so was A.I."

He succeeded in revamping the manufacturing operations, and was rewarded by being put in charge of production at two more of Wrightcraft's aging facilities.

"Maybe my management style was a little rough around the edges, but I think I impressed people because I was always moving. You wouldn't find me in my office very often. If there was a problem somewhere, I made it mine. Even if I didn't have to. It might have been counterproductive sometimes, but I'd rather be on the floor seeing if we could get a piece of equipment back on line than spend time on administration or planning."

People at A.I. were taking notice of the results Bowen achieved. By now he was director of production for all Wrightcraft plants. Management teams were sent to learn how he was working his magic. Bowen was a reluctant teacher.

"They wanted me to explain what I was doing in each operation. Projections. Staff responsibilities. Development. Budgets. Everything. I didn't have time for that. I wasn't running an MBA program, I had work to do."

At 42 Bowen was named senior vice president of operations. His new responsibilities left less time for the hands-on style he enjoyed.

"I missed the old days, but I still kept things hopping. I'd go to the purchasing department and say, 'Next quarter we want to see a five percent reduction of costs,' or I'd go to production and say, 'ten percent less scrap next quarter.' Everybody'd be in a panic when the end of the quarter rolled around because they knew they hadn't made the targets, but it sure kept 'em on their toes!"

At 44 Bowen turned down an offer from A.I. that would have brought him to corporate headquarters and put him in line for a top-level job in the executive suite.

"Maybe I should have accepted it. My wife wanted me to. The way I worked was driving her crazy. The headquarters job would have meant more prestige, opportunities . . . less hectic. I think that was the problem. I knew I'd have to tone down and be more corporate. But at Wrightcraft I could run my own show. I turned it down."

Instead, Bowen was made president of Wrightcraft, now one of A.I.'s most profitable divisions, with thriving subsidiaries of its own. At 49, continuing his freewheeling style, he was named chief executive officer.

"I didn't think too much about retirement. I knew it was coming, but what can you do about it? It's bad enough without thinking about it."

At 56 Bowen was named chairman of Wrightcraft. Retirement came at 62. The day after the last testimonial in his honor, Bowen and his wife left for a three-week vacation in Hawaii.

"I can't remember the last real vacation I'd taken. But what the hell, after a lifetime of work you're supposed to relax, right? Let me tell you, I was out there in paradise climbing the walls!"

Cutting the vacation short, they returned home. Bowen began to experience wild mood swings. Relations with his wife, who expected retirement to be a time of stability, deteriorated. He was drinking heavily. A physical exam revealed his high blood pressure problem had worsened. Advised to "relax," he and his wife planned a trip to the Bahamas, but two days before they were to leave he canceled the vacation.

"I wasn't feeling well, and I was confused. Scared. She was furious."

Four days later, on a Monday following a night of heavy drinking, Bowen had a heart attack. "They used to tell me, 'Slow down or you'll have a heart attack.' So I tried to slow down and look what happened."

POST-CAREER CONSIDERATIONS

Retirement doesn't provide the kind of stress the Reactive Manager gets from his career. No eleventh-hour contract glitches, no sudden plane flights, no organization and budget at his disposal to carry on his reactive ways.

Yes, there are great stresses in retirement, but they are of a much more quiet and desperate type than the Reactive Manager is used to dealing with. Unless he can sublimate or eliminate his stress-driven characteristics, he may face crises beyond his management abilities.

Reactive personalities are prone to stress-related health problems: hypertension and coronary conditions, alcohol and substance abuse.

Management Personality Assessment Tests

With each management personality profile we include a self-assessment test. Each test has 20 statements, which should be scored from one to five, reflecting a scale from "strongly disagree" to "strongly agree." A score of three would reflect a neutral reaction to the statement. Total scores in the 20-60 range indicate an absence of the associated personality characteristic. Scores in the 61-70 range reveal the presence of some characteristics associated with the corresponding management personality. A score in the 71-85 range is a strong indicator of the problematic management personality. Scores in the 86-100 range are manifestations of extreme problematic personalities.

REACTIVE MANAGER ASSESSMENT TEST

1. I'd rather start up a moderately successful operation than administer a very successful one.
2. Good management means responding fast when things go wrong.
3. My "in" box usually has more things than my "out" box.
4. I like to manage by instinct.
5. You need to shake up an organization to keep people on their toes.
6. The real essentials of good management can't be taught.
7. An operation that's running smoothly is an operation that's stagnating.
8. I don't follow a planned schedule.
9. Administration and paperwork are between a nuisance and a necessary evil.
10. You can't get ahead without taking risks.
11. I need to do things my way.
12. I'm an impatient person.
13. Play by the rules, and you won't get very far.
14. I enjoy gambling or games of chance.
15. I'm an aggressive, rather than a conservative, investor.
16. Most coworkers can't keep up with me.
17. I don't enjoy sedentary leisure pursuits.
18. You've got to constantly push people to get them to perform.
19. I'm a much better leader than a follower.
20. The best managers know what needs to be done without being told.

The Company Man

The Company Man is organizationally driven. He has little sense of his own identity, preferring to be identified as part of a larger group. He needs structure, a team, an organized way of approaching problems and doing things. He tends to be rigid, with little room for improvisation, and often views solutions in finite terms. He often resists change, but will subvert himself to the greater good of the organization.

The Company Man has often stayed with one organization throughout his entire professional life. He is not a great innovator, but a very able administrator. Once a policy has been set, few are better at putting it into practice than the Company Man. He rarely sticks his neck out, preferring that others make major decisions. Once they are made he will do his best to support them wholeheartedly.

Even high-ranking, aggressive executives can develop Company Man characteristics through immersion in one company's corporate culture. Almost 60% of the CEOs surveyed by The Conference Board, a major business think tank, had been with their company at least 21 years. Half of them had only worked for one or two other companies. These tendencies can also develop in executives who would switch jobs were it not for the lucrative pension plans and employment contracts that keep them tied to a particular company.

BOB TAYLOR

Bob Taylor joined Warren & Stearns as a management trainee right after graduating from a Midwestern university with a degree in business administration. W&S was a large packaged goods company known for its conservative marketing practices and well-managed operations.

"I always enjoyed being part of things, even when I was growing up. Little League. Boy Scouts. Clubs in school. I didn't care about being the leader, I just wanted to be involved with other people . . . W&S was perfect for me. They had a great management program, and they had the right working atmosphere. They had social activities, picnics, sports teams . . . I felt right at home."

From his first position as assistant to the purchasing manager at one of the W&S plants, Taylor made steady career advances. His management style meshed well with the W&S philosophy. "You knew what was expected of you. They had management down to a science. If it was rolling out a new product or running a sales meeting, we had a procedure for everything. And it worked, too. Some people complained it was too conservative, but hey, you don't get to be W&S's size unless you're doing something right."

In keeping with company policy, Taylor was exposed to a number of management posts in sales, production, marketing and operations.

"I didn't like all the moving around. It was especially tough on my wife and kids. But wherever we went, I knew we were always part of W&S. They did everything they could to help you settle in a new community. They took care of everything."

Taylor's dedication and commitment to the company kept him moving up the corporate ladder. By age 47 he was director of marketing, Midwest, for one of W&S's consumer product lines.

"There was a tremendous feeling of team spirit. Everybody knew what they had to do, and everybody pitched in to get the job done."

At 57 Taylor was named group vice president for consumer marketing for W&S, his final promotion. The company had a mandatory retirement age of 65 for executives in Taylor's position.

"They gave me a great sendoff—the company, my staff—but suddenly I wasn't part of it anymore. I knew those were the company rules, but still, it didn't seem right. I spent my whole career there."

Taylor tried hanging onto the old times as much as possible.

"I kept in touch with the people at the office. I called all the time. After awhile I got the idea they didn't want me calling so often. But I was hoping there was some way I might be able to help. With a company like W&S though, the procedures are all down pat. They didn't need me."

His hobby of photography was incapable of filling the void left by the loss of his career, and Taylor became increasingly morose and directionless. He began to lose weight and had difficulty sleeping. Finally, at his wife's urging, Taylor sought help. (Interestingly, his first choice was group therapy.) After two sessions, the therapist recommended private counseling with a specialist familiar with retirement problems, and Taylor was able to start putting his post-career life together.

POST-CAREER CONSIDERATIONS

The Company Man is poorly prepared for the unstructured challenges of retirement. He will experience difficulty operating from an evolving and self-defined game plan, rather than a game plan whose articles have been codified as organizational faith. He is bewildered by being in charge of all aspects of an operation (his retirement), and has problems making decisions and setting an agenda. He may feel alone and abandoned. Used to thinking of the organization first, he may feel guilty at the emphasis on self that is a necessary part of every successful retirement.

THE COMPANY MAN ASSESSMENT TEST

1. I'd rather administer a very successful operation than start up a moderately successful one.
2. I've had three or less employers in my career, and been with my present company 15 or more years.
3. My "out" box usually has more things than my "in" box.
4. There's little room for improvisation in a well-run company.
5. Frequent staff meetings are important.
6. Good management is making sure nothing goes wrong.
7. My company has very well defined attitudes and practices.
8. Administration and paperwork are key parts of business success.
9. Teamwork is a prerequisite of business success.
10. It's impossible to overplan.
11. There's usually one best way to do things.
12. Most of my social circle is work-related.
13. Company loyalty is a major executive responsibility.
14. Knowing exactly what's expected of you is essential to getting ahead.
15. A chain of command is essential for successful management.
16. Playing hunches can get you in trouble.
17. I feel a great sense of kinship with my company and colleagues.
18. For developing plans and ideas, I prefer brainstorming to working alone.
20. Playing by the rules is the way to get where you want to go.

The Overachiever

The Overachiever is competition-driven. No matter how successful he is, his competitive drive is based on deep-seated feelings of inferiority. He has a need to demonstrate superiority over others as a way of answering subconscious questions about his own worth.

For the Overachiever, success is measured against others, not against internal standards. He needs to be singled out not for a job well done, but for a job done better than anyone else. He needs stroking, recognition, acknowledgment. He is very attuned to office politics, and tends to pay close attention to the pay and perks his peers receive as a means of measuring his status against theirs.

He has a reputation for workaholic tendencies, and usually drives his staff as hard as he drives himself. Other management skills notwithstanding, he has reached the top primarily by dint of his dogged determination to outperform his colleagues on every rung of the corporate ladder.

RICHARD HAVERSON

"I guess I always felt like an outsider."

Richard Haverson was the youngest child of a working-class family in Boston. He excelled in school, and received a full scholarship to an Ivy League university.

"I was very conscious of class differences there. I had a chip on my shoulder about being on a scholarship. Most of the other students came from families with money and power. I knew if I wanted to succeed, these were the people I'd always have to compete against."

After graduating with honors and a degree in economics, Haverson joined the financial department of a New England-based insurance firm. His attitude wasn't "can do," it was "must do," and he quickly established himself as a comer, beginning a rapid ascent up the management ranks. By age 32 he was vice president for institutional services, the "youngest in the company's history." He directed the investments of tens of millions of dollars of the company's assets.

"I drove myself hard. I was usually the first one in in the morning,

and the last one out of the office at night. But that's what you've got
to do if you want to be the best . . . There are so many variables
you've got to stay on top of when you're handling money like that.
And you've got to keep looking over your shoulder at the same time,
because someone's always trying to make you look bad."

Haverson was developing a controversial reputation in the industry. He was considered aggressive, smart and dedicated, though
some found him abrasive and hard to deal with.

"They could say what they wanted about me, but the figures were
there in black and white. That's when I felt successful. Any time
there was a performance review, my numbers came out on top. I
worked my butt off to make sure of that."

Haverson's workaholic tendencies were causing domestic
problems, but he couldn't let up. At 35 he was lured to a plum national position with a rival insurance company.

"It was a different kind of competition. At the regional level you
can always see how you stack up against everybody else. But at national you can't measure yourself the same way. I probably should
have concentrated a little more on the job, and a little less on trying
to figure out how I was doing, but that's just the way I am."

Haverson was now in charge of putting together the financing for
large commercial and industrial construction projects. Under his
stewardship, it became a key sector of his company's business. By
the age of 45 he was considered a major figure by real estate and
construction movers and shakers in the Northeast. But he still felt
like an outsider looking in.

"You've always got your eye on the top spot—that's what
everybody aspires to. I was making lots of money for them, but that
didn't seem to matter as much as where your family was from or
what clubs you belonged to."

At 54 he was named vice chairman, corporate finance.

"I sensed I'd moved up the ladder as far as I was going to. You
hear the scuttlebutt. I was doing a great job, but they didn't think I
was enough of a team player to be president. They gave it to one of
the bluebloods I graduated with. I might have been a failure, but I
wasn't a quitter. I drove myself right up till the end."

Haverson retired, as company policy dictated, at 62.

"My main feeling was worthlessness. Worthlessness and failure.
I'd given everything to get to the top and I didn't make it. I always
gave everything to be the best. Now I wasn't doing anything, so I
couldn't be anything. I had no identity."

Haverson dwelled on his career disappointments, and nurtured resentment toward those he felt had thwarted him. He began to abuse the tranquilizers that had been prescribed to control his anxiety. Relations with his wife, which had been shaky for some time, deteriorated completely. He withdrew into a medicated stupor.

His wife contacted former colleagues, who dispatched a physician to examine Haverson. With his wife's consent, he was admitted to a private detoxification facility, and enrolled in a therapy program. Gradually Haverson recovered, and began dealing with his post-career problems in a constructive way.

POST-CAREER CONSIDERATIONS

Retirement success is essentially a solitary pursuit. The Over-achiever may face devastating problems in retirement when he finds no one to compete against. Those who measure themselves against others and can't find satisfaction in their own accomplishments will find few barometers of performance in retirement. Opportunities for stroking and recognition are few.

With no way to refute subconscious feelings of inferiority or in-adequacy, the Overachiever will have difficulty working through the negative emotions of retirement. He is a prime candidate for depression and stress-related health problems.

THE OVERACHIEVER ASSESSMENT TEST

1. I've got something to prove, and my job is the best way to prove it.
2. Knowing I did well isn't as important as having other people know it.
3. Colleagues are potential adversaries.
4. I'm a sore loser.
5. I'm very conscious of the perks, benefits and salaries of my colleagues.
6. I have an easier time remembering those who hurt me than those who help me.
7. You can't get to the top without playing the office politics game.

8. My career commitment has interfered with my health or personal life.
9. I make it a point to always carry business cards.
10. Winning isn't everything, it's the only thing.
11. The thought of someone getting the best of me in a business deal is very upsetting.
12. Business and pleasure don't mix.
13. The end justifies the means.
14. Few people measure up to my standards.
15. It's not what you know, it's who you know that counts.
16. I'm very concerned with what others think of me.
17. I delegate responsibility, not authority.
18. High visibility is an important part of leadership.
19. I have difficulty working with people I perceive as less competent than I am.
20. Situations can arise making it necessary to sabotage a colleague.

The Combat Vet

The Combat Vet is survival-driven. This problem personality is different from the other three because it only exhibits itself in the latter stages of an executive's career, and results more from career-generated than personality-generated pressures. It's a response to a perceived threat.

The Combat Vet starts out as a raw recruit to the corporate battlefield, eager to succeed. But at some point his career becomes a matter of survival, and the transition can be precipitated by a number of circumstances: a corporate takeover or shakeup that results in a new management team being installed over the executive in question. A merger that results in a clash of corporate cultures. Being passed over for a key promotion. Feeling a career has peaked. Fear of being terminated. Job burnout.

The Combat Vet management style is vintage foxhole. "Keep your head down and your mouth shut" is his philosophy. He's developed a cynical view of corporate machinations, his career and life in general. He may stay holed up in his office/bunker, hiding from the enemy, those higher up the corporate chain of command, and those below him looking for guidance he's no longer able to give. He shows no initiative, and demonstrates extreme passivity regarding both his management responsibilities and his ability to influence his career.

RANDALL RAWLINGS

Randall Rawlings started his career with a bright and positive outlook. Using GI benefits, he got a degree in communications, and went to Los Angeles to work in broadcasting. He wound up in advertising.

"A friend of mine told me about an opening in a local agency. At first I had a negative attitude about advertising. But I needed a job, and I thought I'd give it a try. It turned out to be great work . . . I don't know if I had what it takes to be a big time announcer, anyway."

Rawlings worked for several local agencies, and his enthusiasm and ability helped him transfer to the L.A. office of Sloan Cummings, a Chicago-based agency. At age 37 he was brought to the Chicago office to run a national account.

"I'd heard they were having a lot of problems with the account. The client was unhappy, the agency people were unhappy, but I felt I knew the business from the ground up, and I figured this would be my chance to show my stuff."

Rawlings turned the account around, and was gradually given responsibility for more of the agency's national business. With his extensive background he was able to bring order to Sloan Cummings's regional and headquarters offices.

At 54 he was made senior vice president of operations at Sloan Cummings, and was talked about as potential presidential material. But forces much bigger than Rawlings were at work. The company was losing ground to younger, more aggressive agencies. Rawlings could keep operations running smoothly, but new business wasn't being brought aboard.

"Of course people talked, and we wondered what would happen, but it didn't seem like an irreversible situation. One morning I came in and there was a memo about an urgent management meeting. That's when we found out the agency had been sold."

A large New York agency had acquired Sloan Cummings, and major changes began immediately. "They brought in a new team, a lot of people were fired. I was safe for a while. They knew I was the guy holding everything together. But it wasn't fair. Forget about the presidency, I didn't know if I'd have a job in a couple of months. Let's face it, at 57 I didn't want to be out on the street looking for another job."

Rawlings withdrew into himself.

"I just stayed in my office and made sure I had plenty of paper to push around. One day I'd be worried they were going to fire me; the next I hoped they'd get it over with. There was nothing I could do about it. I decided to just sit back and collect my paycheck. I didn't feel I owed them anything."

At 59 Rawlings was offered an early retirement incentive package, and he took it.

"I was burned out by the whole thing. Seeing good people get fired, the arrogance of the new management. And I felt guilty that I didn't get fired. I felt like a collaborator . . . I was glad it was finally over with, but it seemed like such a waste. That's all I kept thinking about. I couldn't do anything."

For a year and a half Rawlings was unable to motivate himself in a positive direction, and he began exhibiting signs of emotional instability. The retirement plans he and his wife had previously made lay dormant. A chance encounter with a former colleague led him to a community mental health program. He was referred to a private therapist who began helping Rawlings with the task of salvaging his emotional stability. By establishing small goals, he was gradually able to overcome his negative attitudes, reassert himself, and establish a healthy retirement that now includes part-time consulting work.

POST-CAREER CONSIDERATIONS

You can't win a war in a defensive posture. The Combat Vet's passivity is his biggest enemy. His retirement becomes the next theater of war, with "survival" again the goal. While he may survive, his passivity will render him unable to muster the initiative and imagination required for a successful retirement. Shellshocked, he will muddle along, oblivious to the opportunities available to executives who've completed their corporate tours of duty.

The onset of the Combat Vet's retirement problems is usually gradual, rather than dramatically precipitous.

THE COMBAT VET ASSESSMENT TEST

1. I'm concerned about the security of my job.
2. If top management screws things up, there's nothing you can do about it.
3. I don't like my job.
4. I feel my career has reached its peak.
5. I've seen valuable managers and friends dismissed from this company.
6. My company has been involved in a merger or acquisition within the last two years.
7. Sometimes I feel like I'm just collecting a paycheck.
8. I often dread going to work in the morning.
9. This company doesn't appreciate me, and I don't care what happens to it once I'm gone.
10. One of my top management priorities is managing to keep my job.
11. There's little challenge in my work, and I don't see the point of putting any effort into it.
12. I have a hard time forgetting career disappointments.
13. I'm not as motivated as I used to be.
14. The reality is, people have very little control over their lives.
15. There's been a management shakeup above me within the last two years.
16. I've given more than I've gotten from my career.
17. If I could do it all over again, I'd do it a lot differently.
18. Company morale is very low.
19. When I look back over my career, I feel little satisfaction.
20. I'm prone to feelings of guilt, despair and depression.

Personality Overview

The case histories we've presented are extreme examples. You don't have to be a full-blown Reactive Manager, Company Man, Overachiever or Combat Vet to possess some of the characteristics and face some of the problems unique to each. Think about your attitudes and behavior, and see if they indicate the presence of any of these potentially unhealthy motivations. If so, be ready to deal with them.

We'll show you the management skills that can help you do this, and tell you how to adapt them for the retirement transition at the office and at home. We'll talk about the wealth of post-career options that await, and how you can take advantage of them and achieve retirement success.

CHAPTER THREE

THE REVAMPING OF RETIREMENT AND THE EXECUTIVE RETIREMENT MANAGEMENT CONCEPT

Six Trends Reshaping Retirement

In the past, the typical maturing manager worked until mandatory retirement somewhere between the ages of 62 and 65, and settled down to a sunset existence. There were few outlets for the skills, abilities and knowledge the retiree had developed over a lifetime. He was supposed to keep quiet, if not completely fade away, and "act his age" in keeping with societal expectations. Things have changed dramatically. Some of the changes have been swift and tumultuous, others are occurring more slowly but have no less of an impact. Your job is to be familiar with these six trends, and make your post-career plans with these options and opportunities in mind. They are:

1. The rise of early retirement

2. Evolving mandatory retirement policies
3. Growing post-career employment opportunities
4. Increased executive health and fitness
5. Growing financial vitality
6. A new image of the mature

THE RISE OF EARLY RETIREMENT

Early retirement is now an accepted option for executives. (This is one of the most important trends reshaping retirement, and is treated more extensively in Chapter 7.) The average age of retirement is edging downward; it is currently 62 and declining. There are early retirement incentive offers as a result of corporate belt-tightening or M&A activity. More pension plans now have built-in incentives that let managers retire with sizable benefits before traditional retirement age. Liberated attitudes about leisure, and expanded post-career employment opportunities, have led many executives to leave their first career long before traditional retirement age, even in the absence of any external incentive.

Early retirement issues need careful evaluation. Executives need to consider if it's a viable alternative for them, how to size up an early retirement package, when they should turn down an attractive offer, and what to do when and if they elect to exercise this option.

EVOLVING MANDATORY RETIREMENT POLICIES

Mandatory retirement is now, for most employees, illegal. While statutory protection doesn't apply to executives in so-called "policy making" positions (defined by law as those whose retirement compensation exceeds $44,000 annually), many companies have banned mandatory retirement altogether, regardless of position. Others only apply it to their most senior corporate officers, and sometimes provide executives the option of shifting down to a less exalted position.

Increasingly, executives have to think ahead and consider when and if they *want* to leave their jobs, not when they *have* to. Yet even in the absence of mandatory retirement, corporate culture often dictates retirement for top executives—it's an unwritten rule. Executives have to be familiar with their companies' policies, both written and unwritten, and evaluate their impact. They may have to consider transferring to a company whose long range commitment to them is more in keeping with their own desires, or start planning on when to step aside in the absence of corporate compulsion.

GROWING POST-CAREER EMPLOYMENT OPPORTUNITIES

More and more, retirement is a springboard to new employment opportunities. It's becoming commonplace for executives to channel their skills into new careers. Hobbies are transformed into small businesses. Education provides the entrance into an entirely new area of work. Management expertise is fashioned into thriving consultancies. Some executives take up low-pressure, part-time jobs, others retain scaled-back ties to their companies. There are as many options as there are maturing managers.

An executive needs to know his interests and abilities, and know which post-career employment avenues are viable. He has to be thoroughly familiar with himself to avoid making costly mistakes, like plunging into a second career because everyone else is doing it, or following a pie-in-the-sky plan to start his own business when he'd be happier following a more traditional retirement lifestyle.

Retirement Management (which includes thorough research and planning and begins well before retirement) is essential to evaluate the available options and decide which are best on an individual basis.

INCREASED EXECUTIVE HEALTH AND FITNESS

The stunning strides in life expectancy made in this century are well-documented, but they only tell part of the story of the new vitality of the mature. People aren't only living longer, they're living healthier. A U.S. Census Bureau report found that four out of five people over the age of 65 rate their health as "good" or "excellent." Those who report chronic illness may suffer from nothing more than weakening eyesight or mild arthritis.

Age is no longer a barrier to vigorous physical activity of any sort, and executives are enjoying a more active retirement. They run in marathons, climb mountains, bicycle and box. Increased corporate and personal emphasis on executive health means managers are taking charge of their bodies, entering their mature years fit and filled with vitality. Improved health creates a greater variety of physical activities that can become enjoyable leisure pursuits, and active programs of retirement health management can maximize these opportunities and benefits.

GROWING FINANCIAL VITALITY

Today's manager has greater financial wherewithal to make his post-career dreams come true. The 50+ market, more than 60 million strong, has more disposable income than any other age group in the United States. Homes are paid for, and children have been educated. Those between the ages of 55 and 65 enjoy the highest per capita income in the United States, while those between 65 and 75 have the highest average assets per capita. A proliferation of generous pension and profit-sharing programs, corporate financial planning assistance, and a growing financial sophistication means executives are leaving the work force with more money than ever before. Those who plan ahead can use this capital for a firm financial foundation on which to build a successful future.

A NEW IMAGE OF THE MATURE

Along with the concrete changes, tremendously powerful ones are taking place in the collective consciousness. We're witnessing a fundamental alteration of the public's and the executive's image of the maturing individual. The idea of the retiree as over the hill and in the way is being shattered by the ascendancy of dynamic and vibrant seniors. Our idea of what constitutes "old" is changing. A 1974 Harris poll asked people at what age the average person becomes old. Men said 63, women said 62. Seven years later, the same question garnered responses of 66 and 65.

In movies and books and on television, the infatuation with youth is being replaced by an interest in maturity. Our sex symbols and icons of yesterday retain their allure today. Paul Newman is over 60. Gloria Steinem has passed 50. Sociologists talk of "an age-irrelevant" society and "youth creep," as older gets younger. This changing perception is opening more avenues that were formerly blocked by outdated stereotypes of the mature as doddering and ineffectual. Age is no longer a barrier to virtually any endeavor.

The Five Principles of Executive Retirement Management

Despite the "easier times" for America's mature, preparing for retirement is a big job. You must martial all your mental and physical resources to negotiate the retirement transition, and get the most out of your retirement potential. How do you do it? By putting your management skills to work!

Without management skills, the executive is nothing more than a man or woman in a suit, and a company is only an aimless amalgamation of possibilities. More than 4 billion dollars a year is spent in the United States on managerial training, to improve executive performance and knowledge. That figure doesn't include salaries of in-house trainers, or the cost of man-hours spent undergoing this education. But there's a sense that the value and usefulness of these skills ends when a manager's career does. That notion is now obsolete. The decisions, emotions and options facing executives during retirement demand that management skills be used to achieve post-career success.

This is the basis of executive retirement management.

1.   Retirement is a career.
2.   A successful retirement requires work.
3.   Retirement success is different from career success.
4.   Management skills have a vital role in retirement success.
5.   Management skills must be modified to meet the challenges of retirement.

RETIREMENT IS A CAREER

No wonder so many executives have fared poorly in retirement; they've been brainwashed by talk of "golden sunset years" and "taking it easy." They impose no direction on their life, and find themselves adrift. Forget that! You need to take a strategic and dynamic view of retirement. When you can't find direction, when you can't define goals or find the energy to work toward them, then retirement becomes a failure.

Whether you want to start your own company or lie in a hammock, retirement, like a career, needs a structure, a function, a defined purpose and an agenda. Within this environment, objectives can be set, management skills exercised and results assessed. This provides the growth environment necessary for post-career success.

A SUCCESSFUL RETIREMENT REQUIRES WORK

This is another reason many executives founder in retirement—they equate the end of working in a career with the end of work in their lives. They don't make the effort to be successful. Overseeing the retirement transition, adapting management skill, and overcoming emotional turmoil takes work and commitment. It's some of the most satisfying work you'll ever find, but it is work. You have to muster determination, patience and strength to make the most of the future. The more ambitious your plans, the more management responsibilities you'll have. Be ready to apply yourself fully. It took years of schooling and training to prepare you for your career. Retirement management also requires education, training and homework. There *are* executives who have no trouble finding post-career fulfillment, but they're in the minority.

RETIREMENT SUCCESS IS DIFFERENT
FROM CAREER SUCCESS

Career success is easy to measure; advancement up a corporate ladder, bigger titles and responsibilities, more pay and perks, a corner office. These tangible barometers of achievement are hard to replace. In retirement there's little stroking, you don't earn recognition for a job well done or add to a financial bottom line. Unless you change your view of success, you'll subconsciously look for the same kinds of reward. You need alternative yardsticks of achievement. Personal standards must be asserted over institutional ones. Even in a working retirement, be it a second career, part-time work or consulting, enjoyment and fulfillment should be what you work toward, not the financial and titular goals you've pursued during your career.

Retirement success isn't something that can be summed up in a sentence or a phrase, because the elements of retirement success are different for each executive. But there are overall guidelines to keep in mind.

Retirement success is:

Having a clear idea of the lifestyle you want to lead, and the ability
   to work toward achieving it.
Feeling involved and growing.
Maintaining your health.
Being comfortable in the knowledge your career is behind you, and
   looking forward to all that lies ahead.

Retirement success is not:

An ill-defined plan to "take it easy."
A crash fitness program to convince yourself you're still young.
Feeling it's all downhill from here.
Brooding over career disappointments.
Looking backward instead of forward.
Endless rounds of golf because there's nothing else to do.
A schedule packed with unfulfilling activities.

MANAGEMENT SKILLS HAVE A VITAL ROLE IN RETIREMENT SUCCESS

Executives who want a healthy and rewarding retirement need to apply management skills to the job. Planning for the future and preparing for new challenges requires a full range of the same skills used to achieve career success.

Retirement management isn't to be confused with "keeping busy." A business couldn't survive if key people squandered their time on busy work, meaningless tasks that give the appearance of involvement. Activity level isn't a gauge of the vibrancy of your retirement career. What's important is engaging in activities that have meaning for you. It's a matter of quality of activities, not quantity. The successful retiree isn't judged by a busy schedule, but by real commitment to enjoyable pursuits engaged in without pressure. Putting your management skills to work will help you identify and achieve meaningful goals.

MANAGEMENT SKILLS MUST BE MODIFIED TO MEET THE CHALLENGES OF RETIREMENT

The challenges of retirement are different from the challenges of a career. Management skills have to be adapted to these new challenges. Since no two managers will have identical post-career plans and problems, they can't have the same solutions.

Applying management skills in a career requires an institutional approach, "homogenization"; tasks and operational methods are reduced to basics, so they can be performed by any number of people. In retirement you practice personal management, "individualization"—expanding the role of the individual, developing operating principles and methods unique to your needs. The individual is no longer subverted for the good of the organization; the individual *is* the organization.

The degree of adaptation of management skills is directly related to the difference between your career and post-career lifestyles. A radical change, from a high-powered, hard-charging lifestyle to one of enforced relaxation (e.g., for medical reasons) requires lots of adaptation. So can a move to another city. The executive who slides into a second career very similar to his current one won't need to modify these skills as much.

The trends reshaping retirement discussed in the first part of this chapter are a fact of every executive's life, and affect each individual differently. Applying the principles of executive retirement management to these forces is the key to controlling their impact on *your* future.

CHAPTER FOUR

MANAGEMENT SKILLS, EXECUTIVE CAREER STYLES, AND RETIREMENT

Management is being transformed from an art into a science. What seemed like hocus pocus in achieving business success has been revealed to be a set of finite skills that can be applied to an infinite number of management objectives. In order to manage your retirement successfully, there are seven key management skills you must command:

1. Creativity
2. Analysis
3. Communication
4. Planning
5. Implementation
6. Flexibility
7. Administration

All these skills are used together. Think of them as an interlocking web of abilities. Creativity helps you with planning.

Communication assists implementation. Analysis identifies administrative needs. We stated at the outset that few executives applied all these skills adequately in retirement. But they can be developed.

Following is a series of skill assessments and exercises. Try thinking of how you can apply all seven skills to each set of exercises, and you'll see how these skills work together. If you're deficient in a particular skill, work on improving it. Create your own skill exercise plan. Use the skills you're strong in to help develop the ones you're weak in.

As you work through your retirement transition, turn back to these skill assessments periodically to check your progress.

Retirement Management Skills Assessments

In an era of specialization, one manager concentrates on strategic planning, another is charged with turning plans into reality, a third has responsibility for checking up on the first two managers. But for effective retirement management, executives need to be able to exercise all seven of these skills. Together, they'll be used to chart your future, establish a timetable for realizing goals and monitoring progress. They'll help you think about your future early in your career, negotiate your retirement transition, and manage your life when your career is over.

We'll describe each, provide an assessment test to help you gauge the degree to which you currently possess these skills, and list exercises to assist in their development.

Each assessment test has 10 statements. Each should be scored on a scale of 1-5, indicating responses from strongly disagree to strongly agree. A neutral response should be graded 3. The higher the score, the stronger the skill. Scores of 41-50 indicate extreme competency. Scores between 31-40 show adequate skill; 21-30 indicates a definite need for improvement; and scores in the 10-20 range reveal a serious deficiency.

CREATIVITY

Many managers are suspicious of creativity. They think of it as a wild animal, something that can be dangerous if it gets loose. This perception isn't helped by the stereotype image of the "creatives" in the business organization—unpredictable, disheveled, self-indulgent. This pigeonholing of creativity helps to atrophy creative abilities in executives up and down the management ranks. The act of designating one class of workers as "creatives," or one area as the "creative department," automatically sends the message that everyone else is uncreative, further eroding the confidence of managers in their creative abilities.

Creativity is simply the ability to use your imagination, to maintain a fresh perspective on problems and solutions, to see things in new ways. Successful managers are creative, and so are successful retirees. By remaining creative, they see new possibilities and opportunities. Curiosity and a zest for life are part of creativity, while complacency dulls the creative spirit. Developing new interests stimulates creativity and helps avoid stagnation.

Creativity can help you decide what you want to do with your future. Imagine you had all the money in the world. What would you be doing? Someone who says "I'd like to own the biggest yacht in the world and go sailing," is obviously interested in boating. But you don't need the biggest yacht in the world to satisfy an interest in boating. Often, it's the accoutrements and trappings of an activity we focus on more than the activity itself. Think creatively, and you'll see similar scenarios are in reach. There are affordable ocean cruises, you can buy a smaller yacht, or charter a sloop to sail around the Bahamas sometime.

Creativity Adaptation

Managers like to talk about "creative solutions," but many of them never give the concept any more than lip service. Creativity needs nurturing. You need to unleash your imagination from the "rational" constraints many executives chain it to. Too many things have to be justified, have to make sense, have to add up. There's a bottom line in black and white. That's not what creativity is about. Be prepared to devote time to exercising your imagination, like you would your body. You can develop your creativity in the same way. Think of things you like to do now. Things you used to like to do. New things you've never done but want to try. Imagine yourself engaging in different activities and leading different lifestyles.

An executive with a consumer products company wanted to improve his creativity. Actually, he wasn't sure what creativity was, and wanted to know if he had any of it. He arranged to get together with top people from his company's ad agency creative department one afternoon to talk about how they developed their ideas. They talked about a person's future as a product, and brainstormed on different ways to approach it. Seeing this process firsthand, and participating in it, made him feel much more comfortable wearing a "creative" hat of his own, and gave him valuable ideas on how to harness his creativity.

> "Large bureaucracies like this one have difficulty promoting imagination and creativity."
> —Robert Gates, CIA Deputy Director of Intelligence

Creativity Skills Assessment

1. If an item comes with instructions for operation or assembly, I try to figure it out for myself first.
2. I like to think of myself as an idea person.
3. I would rather make something I design myself than build something from a set of plans.
4. I try to avoid routine ways of doing things.
5. In public places, I imagine about the lives of people I see.
6. I have a hobby, like music, sculpting or writing, that involves artistic improvisation.
7. I may become absentminded and totally absorbed when I'm involved in an interesting project.
8. I don't like dress codes and/or rigid working hours.
9. I'm comfortable taking part in brainstorming sessions aimed at developing new ideas.
10. When it comes to pleasure reading, I prefer fiction to non-fiction.

Creativity Exercises

1. Think of a kitchen or yard appliance that doesn't exist that would make your life easier.
2. Imagine you live in a home 100 years in the future. What does it look like outside, and what's on the inside?
3. Make up a one-page story about an executive facing retirement.
4. Think of at least 10 things you can use a brick for.
5. Imagine you're the lead character in a book. What kind of book is it? Outline a happy ending.

ANALYSIS

The ability to size up a situation, identify its components, and determine the effect of variables on the overall equation, is a requisite of business success. All the facts in the world won't help if you can't sort through them and put them back together cogently so you can see what direction they point to. In the business world, fact-finding missions, statistics, financial and production targets can make us forget the importance of "soft" issues like analysis. Judgment is based on analysis. When you hear about a project that went awry, even though the numbers were right, the marketing surveys all positive, it usually means there was a lapse in analysis. Indeed, our ever-increasing ability to measure a dizzying array of minutiae, computerized financial forecasting, and other feats of technical prowess tend to diminish attention paid to figuring out what it all means.

In both business and personal life, analysis is often hampered by our proximity to the situation. We're too close to the problem, too involved to step back and get the big picture—the "can't see the forest for the trees" syndrome. We attempt to find a solution without every properly defining the problem.

Analysis Adaptation

Sound analysis in the corporate environment is predominantly impersonal; the struggle is to keep personal feelings from analysis and decision making. In retirement, the challenge is the opposite: to analyze situations from a personal perspective. To help with post-career analysis, remember the bottom line is satisfaction with your life. You have the freedom and latitude to make decisions that fly in the face of "objective" reasoning, as long as you've analyzed the situation from a personal point of view.

The lack of black and white standards of post-career success can also make analyzing problems and objectives a difficult proposition. Whether or not an executive properly applies analysis in his career, the problems he focuses on are often concrete: X number of widgets need to be sold by a certain date; a decision on whether a new plant has to be built must be made; ways to cut the costs of an expensive manufacturing process must be developed. Figuring out the best way to accomplish these goals calls for analysis.

Establish clear-cut goals in your post-career life, and you'll find it easier to exercise your analysis skills. But don't reserve analysis for only major decisions and goal setting. Even everyday activities can use this kind of scrutiny. A manufacturing sales representative who enjoyed golfing during his career decided to cut way back on his game in retirement—after he analyzed his involvement and realized his favorite part of his time on the links was entertaining clients and making deals, not swatting the golf ball.

Analysis Skills Assessment
1. Once I undertake a project, I'm rarely caught by unforeseen problems.
2. I like to examine an issue from all sides and form my own opinion before soliciting opinions from others.
3. I have no trouble wading through voluminous reports and getting to the heart of the issue.
4. I like brainteasers, crosswords and mental puzzles.
5. I put time and research into my investments.
6. If things aren't working out according to plan, I can usually figure out why.
7. I've made it a point to learn all facets of my company's business.
8. I like to look for ways to improve procedures.
9. I know my goals for the future.
10. I understand each member of my family, and how we all relate to each other.

Analysis Exercises
1. Think of your three greatest career successes. What enabled you to achieve them?
2. Identify five major goals of yours. What are the factors that could help you achieve them?
3. Gather three kinds of flowers. Analyze the smell of each, and write down your thoughts. Note the differences without making qualitative judgments or comparisons.
4. Write down what you anticipate will be your five biggest adjustment problems in retirement, and a strategy for dealing with each of them.
5. Picture an idealized, yet plausible post-career lifestyle. Write a one-page paper describing it.

COMMUNICATION

Being able to transmit and receive information, express a point of view, and engage in a give-and-take dialogue with others is an important management skill. Communication is necessary to get everybody working toward the same goals, and for facilitating the flow of information necessary for optimal performance. In an era of enlightened management, executives are expected to know the why as well as the how of their jobs. In many ways, the trend to reduce layers of management is as much about facilitating communication as it is about cutting payrolls. Corporations now realize that the importance of communication doesn't end at the company parking lot exit. The growing importance of corporate communications and public relations offices is a recognition of the need for this skill. Companies pay a high price for poor communication. Business reversals, public relations disasters—a tremendous waste of money and effort can easily result from communication lapses. And this skill is just as important in personal life.

Communication Adaptation
In the home environment, communication isn't merely a matter of talking. It's an involved sharing of thoughts, feelings, concerns, even anger. Without communication people drift apart, relationships wither and die. If you think your communication skills have atrophied in your relationship with your family, make an effort to exercise and improve them.

Personal communication is also important to the retirement transition in the office. You've got to be comfortable discussing issues with personnel officers and others in the position to provide information about benefits, company retirement training, and other hard facts of retirement. You may have concerns about soft issues, like adjusting to a new identity, or developing leisure activities. Without communication, these unaddressed worries and fears feed upon themselves.

A successful retirement is a cooperative venture, and communication is the skill that allows cooperative plans to be developed. Your new lifestyle may be acceptable to you but not to your spouse. Or your own expectations may not be met, without your having a handle on the reason. Communication gets you external input and provides you with a sounding board for ideas.

Communication also forces you to articulate plans and make vague agendas concrete. It makes possible the consensus you will need for the team effort that will help make your post-career future a success.

An executive commuted frequently between his company's Midwestern headquarters and a manufacturing plant on the West Coast. A soft-spoken man, as retirement approached he felt concerned about an inability to discuss important issues about the future with his wife, friends or company officials. He didn't want to get involved with therapy, thinking that would be making too much of a problem than was really there. The solution? He found a counselor on the West Coast he felt comfortable with, and saw him on some of his business trips, just to talk things over. The distance from those close to him made it easier for him to open up, and the intermittent counseling fit in with his self-image of the informal assistance he needed. After several visits, he began overcoming his reticence about discussing these same issues at home.

Communication Skills Assessment
1. I rarely feel misinterpreted or misunderstood.
2. If something's on my mind, I let people know about it.
3. I have an outgoing and open personality.
4. I keep my people informed, either in person, by memo or as an operating philosophy.
5. I'm as good at listening as I am at talking.
6. When making plans, I solicit input from others, at home and at the office.
7. At home, we discuss issues that are important to the family.
8. I encourage my people to discuss work and personal problems with me.
9. There is someone I feel comfortable discussing personal matters with.
10. My colleagues and I freely share important information.

Communication Exercises
1. Discuss a memorable vacation, and what you and your family liked best about it.
2. Select a movie or television show you and someone close to you want to see. After seeing it, spend one hour discussing it.
3. Talk to a friend about hobbies and things you liked to do as youngsters.

4. With your spouse or a friend your age, exchange a list of five things you'd like to do in retirement.
5. Pick a sitcom on TV. Watch it with your spouse or friend with the sound off. Pretend the characters are talking about retirement issues or a similar theme, and make up the dialogue of what they're saying.

PLANNING

The ability to develop a workable agenda, a sound program for achieving your goals, to set a course of action to get you where you want to go is essential for success. Planning gives you a framework to work from, a blueprint, a road map. It helps identify potential problems and formulate solutions.

The level of planning you demonstrate in your career is fairly easy to gauge. How thoroughly do you prepare for meetings, reports and negotiations? Do you prefer to "wing it," trust gut instinct and a feeling for the situation at hand? Are you always "under the gun" as a deadline approaches, or do you develop workable schedules for accomplishing tasks? Do you develop long-range goals and a plan for achieving them? No matter what level of planning you currently exhibit, make plans now to put this skill to work in retirement.

Planning Adaptation

Business planning is usually based on rapidly changing, elastic and highly volatile situations; a complex interaction of people and events. What's the reaction to an initial offer? Will exchange rates change enough overnight to justify an international transaction? Important decisions sometimes have to be put off until the last minute and, once made, are frequently irrevocable. This creates an approach to planning at variance with the demands of retirement. Be ready to make adjustments for retirement planning. You won't have late-breaking developments to react to; you won't be stuck with the consequences of decisions that can't be reversed.

Examine the level of planning you demonstrate in your personal life. Personal plans often ride on the coattails of professional plans, so it becomes easy to neglect establishing non-career goals. Career priorities take precedence over personal ones. Where you move to, when you vacation, are often dictated by career plans and responsibilities. Without an external agenda imposing order on your life, planning becomes more open-ended, harder to grasp. The range of alternatives can be too overwhelming for those who aren't prepared.

Preparing for contingencies is as important in personal planning as in the business world. Subject plans to best- and worst-case scenarios. This helps you spot opportunities and avoid unpleasant surprises. Once you uncover danger areas ahead, you can give them a wide berth, or be ready to respond to them constructively.

In making retirement plans, executives frequently feel more at the mercy of events over which they have no control than they do in their business world. In retirement, unpleasant contingencies are much more avoidable, and you're the only one who can put yourself out of business.

Make your plans challenging. It keeps you on your toes and deters complacency. Avoid making things too comfortable and predictable, but don't make unreasonable demands on yourself.

Get planning help from others. In your career you have input from colleagues in developing plans, interjecting practical considerations and providing a sounding board for ideas (as discussed under communication skills). Develop a planning network for retirement, too. Bring others into the picture and expose plans to the same kind of feedback that's so useful to business planning.

One high-level manager of a mid-sized company who had trouble thinking about planning from a post-career perspective went to his office on a Saturday, when he knew it would be empty. Wandering the empty halls, and observing the serenity that enveloped the usually busy area, had a profound effect on him. He wasn't able to grasp his thoughts completely, but it helped convince him not only that he'd have to plan for the future, but also that his planning would be somewhat different than he was used to in his company's usually boisterous environs.

Planning Skills Assessment
1. My management responsibilities include strategic planning, product development or other long-range objectives.
2. My vacations are well planned.
3. My leisure and weekend time is carefully allotted to activities I enjoy.
4. I have well-defined career goals.
5. I develop a workable agenda for achieving objectives.

6. I maintain a list of "things to do" for errands and household projects.
7. I've started formulating realistic post-career plans.
8. I can accurately gauge how long it will take to complete various projects, both at the office and at home.
9. I'm never behind schedule on projects I'm responsible for.
10. My schedule or date book accurately reflects how I spend my time.

Planning Exercises
1. Imagine the following scenario: You've just received a large windfall, and been told you can't work anymore. Write a one-page paper on what you would do.
2. Devote two evenings during an upcoming week to discussing post-career plans with your spouse and/or others who are close to you.
3. Imagine you were going to fulfill a lifelong dream: hiking around the world, climbing Mount Everest or starting your own business. Write down a ten-step plan for how you would accomplish this dream.
4. Evaluate the difference between the planning you demonstrate in your career and in your personal life. List five suggestions for improving performance in both areas.
5. Get a schedule book similar to what you use at work. Create an ideal one-week schedule that includes all your favorite non-career activities. Include the restaurants you'd want to dine in, the places you'd want to go, the things you'd want to do.

IMPLEMENTATION

After your dreams have been converted into plans, implementation is the skill that turns them into reality. This is the ability to get the job done once it's been defined.

Implementation is a key executive skill. Managers enjoy accomplishment, and there's usually an immediate display of results when implementation is the skill being exercised. A number of adulatory designations indicate our regard for the manager with strong implementation skills: a "go-getter," a "man of action," a "can-do" executive.

Implementation Adaptation

Many executives have difficulty with implementation skills in retirement. They're used to having an army of people at their disposal to help get the job done, and to provide encouragement and a shared sense of purpose. Others are accustomed to leaving implementation efforts to subordinates, essentially delegating the potential blame or success, while they turn their attention to the next problem or project. Reporting the retirement of an electronics industry CEO recently, one newspaper mentioned his reputation as that of "one who seems to have thousands of ideas but has had trouble carrying them out." Even being able to rely on one secretary or assistant can have a significant impact on post-career implementation. Managers forget the legwork and tedious detail work that many projects require. And there's little external pressure to get the job done in retirement. Colleagues notice if projects aren't getting completed at the office, but who's going to know if you don't take that adult education course, don't get involved in an interesting business opportunity you've looked into, or don't take a trip you've planned?

To compensate for the camaraderie of group effort, talk up your efforts to friends and family. Articulating your goals will help you reach for them, and letting others know about them will generate enthusiasm from external sources. Build intermediate goals into your implementation efforts to provide a way to gauge accomplishment.

If you're having difficulty implementing your plans, try to identify the reasons. Does the job you've laid out for yourself have enough challenge? Are your implementation goals too ambitious or demanding? Are you having difficulty motivating yourself? Examine the plans themselves. Don't be afraid to revise them. There's no embarrassment in scaling back expectations. Remember, your goal should be to get the most out of your life, and your implementation efforts should be aimed at achieving this end.

The marketing director of a small electrical manufacturer knew she performed at her peak when faced with projects that had a definite beginning, middle and end, rather than, say, an ongoing sales program. She used this knowledge to good advantage by making sure definitive goals were part of her post-career agenda, identifying when implementation of her projects had been successfully completed.

Implementation Skills Assessment
1. My management responsibilities include operational duties, product roll-outs, conducting status reports, and keeping tabs on work-in-progress.
2. I successfully complete all projects assigned to me, whether I encounter problems or not.
3. I consider myself a highly motivated self-starter.
4. Procrastination has never been a problem with me.
5. I'm willing to endure attention to detail if that's what a job calls for.
6. Items on my list of "things to do" are promptly taken care of.
7. I never get notices of past-due bills.
8. I reciprocate on social obligations without delay.
9. There are few projects around the house that get discussed without my acting upon them.
10. I enjoy doing errands and attending to personal business.

Implementation Exercises
1. The next Saturday you are home, locate one thing that can be fixed or improved with a phone call or two hours of work (new shrub planted, buying photo album for vacation pictures, etc.). Get it done.
2. Go to the library or bookstore and get three books on any subject that interests you.
3. List five friends you haven't been in touch with for six months or more. Over the next month, talk to each of them.
4. Buy a subscription to a magazine whose subject is unconnected with your work, but interests you.
5. The next project you delegate to a subordinate, leave one or two of the routine tasks to handle yourself.
6. Within the next two weeks, attend at least one leisure event (e.g., lecture, ball game, play, movie).
7. Write down three things to do you've been putting off. Get them done.
8. If your secretary places your calls, make them yourself one morning.

FLEXIBILITY

If you're ready to meet changing conditions, are quick on your feet and roll with the punches, you're flexible. Uncertainty is a given in the business world, and managers need to be adaptable. There are changing market conditions, questions of suppliers, competitive pressures. Those locked into rigid ways of doing things are the first to fall. More than ever, companies are adopting a lean and mean profile, ready to respond to changing conditions. The trend towards "intrapreneuring," more management autonomy, flex time, sabbaticals and other changes indicates the realization that allowing individuals more room for flexibility and personal development benefits the corporation. The process of switching from career to personal goals is an executive's ultimate exercise in flexibility.

Flexibility Adaptation

High-powered executives can design a work environment that can reduce their need for flexibility. They implement procedures that reflect "their way" of doing things; if they're not as catered to at home, they have their escape at the office. Subordinates change for them, not vice-versa. This can sabotage retirement. You'll encounter a world of change, and you've got to be adaptable to handle your changed schedule, altered finances and new lifestyle. You'll find things rarely work out exactly as you expected right from the start. Flexibility gives you the ability to change your plans, or react to new conditions, instead of giving in to despair and anger.

But there's more to flexibility than just expecting the unexpected. It's also a matter of avoiding routine and complacency. During your career, new projects and responsibilities keep you from getting into a rut; there's always a new challenge. Developing a flexible lifestyle will help you keep this element of challenge in retirement. Flexibility means trying new things, altering your routines and the way you think about things. It means avoiding stagnation.

A former oil company manager had planned and implemented what seemed like an ideal retirement. He and his wife lived on a palatial estate in Virginia, and everyday he pursued his various hobbies. He swam in the morning, went riding, and most afternoons played tennis. They typically hosted at least one small cocktail or dinner party a week. They had it very good, and they were bored. The upshot was that the two of them leased a Winnebago, and set off to drive around the country for what turned out to be six months. They made it a point to stay in modest lodgings whenever possible, just to get away from their pampered lifestyle.

They had a marvelous time, but nonetheless were happy to return home after taking a break to do something different. They vowed to do something adventurous and different whenever they feel complacency's getting the best of them in the future.

You don't have to go on a six-month trip to remain flexible. Small changes, like trying new activities, minor home improvements or a weekend getaway, can keep you looking at life as the ever unfolding adventure it is.

Flexibility Skills Assessment

1. I've had a wide variety of responsibilities and management experience in my career.
2. My job stresses innovation, new concepts and products, rather than repetitive procedures.
3. I can easily change the way I do things to accommodate changing conditions.
4. If I have to change weekend activities due to weather or other circumstances, I easily find something else to do.
5. When I decide to see a movie, watch TV or go to a play, there's usually a variety of possibilities I'm interested in.
6. My spouse and I have dissimilar views, but we compromise on points of contention.
7. The thought of relocating for career or personal reasons isn't troublesome to me.
8. If my favorite product is out of stock, or my first choice on a menu is unavailable, I easily find a substitute.
9. I try to avoid routine in my professional and personal life.
10. If things don't work out or live up to my expectations, I'm able to take it in stride.

Flexibility Exercises

1. Dine in a restaurant you've never eaten in before.
2. Use a different route or mode of transportation than you usually use to get to the office.
3. Make a compromise with someone on an issue that's been a point of contention between you, either at work or at home.
4. Watch a movie or a TV program you don't want to see. Afterwards, write down five things you liked about it.
5. Order a dish you've never tried before at your favorite restaurant.

ADMINISTRATION

Love it or hate it, paperwork and follow-up are part of being a manager. There are reports to read and write, figures to update and review, proposals to outline. Looking forward to kissing this detail work goodbye? Don't plan on it. Post-career administration keeps you on top of all aspects of your operation. It's important for two reasons:

1. Personal administration creates a feeling of control over the post-career environment.
2. Administrative oversight provides a framework for keeping tabs on post-career success and problem areas.

Checking your budget, keeping tabs on investments, reviewing insurance policies—all contribute to a feeling of knowing what's going on in your life, of being in charge. It's an important way of maintaining a positive outlook about your future and your ability to control it. Through administration, you can monitor and evaluate post-career planning and procedures, and assess your application of retirement management skills.

Administration Adaptation

During a career, administrative needs make themselves clear. Papers that show up in the "in" box are expected to find their way to the "out" box. Correspondence has to be kept up with, subordinates have to be evaluated, status reports filed. In retirement, the need for the oversight this paperwork represents isn't as obvious. Yet without it, you may fall prey to irrational fears about money because you haven't adequately kept tabs on finances. A health problem may get out of hand because you're not monitoring your physical well-being. Or you may be paying premiums on insurance policies that no longer fit your needs.

The key to administration in retirement is the same as it often is in your career-paperwork. By committing plans and thoughts to paper, and organizing financial records, insurance policies and other vital documents, you're in an excellent position periodically to review and update information.

Soon after a retired executive's wife left her teaching position they began squabbling over finances. She accused him of being a miser whose tightfisted policies were costing them many opportunities for enjoyment. He accused her of being a spendthrift whose extravagant desires would soon land them both in the poorhouse. Finally, they decided to get an expert third party to examine their finances (which, as we'll talk about later, they should have done well before they retired). This independent evaluation gave them a detailed account of their financial cushion, and, more important, provided a way to track their spending and investments so they felt completely comfortable about what they could and couldn't afford. They still squabble sometimes, but rarely about finances.

Administrative Skills Assessment

1. Administration is a major part of my job responsibilities.
2. My personal papers, insurance policies and investments are organized and well ordered.
3. If I delegate a project, I keep tabs on it as it moves to completion.
4. Reports and paperwork I'm responsible for are promptly taken care of.
5. I always read the fine print before I make a purchase or sign a document.
6. I've never needed an extension to complete my tax returns.
7. We keep a tight rein on our household budget, and know what our expenses are.
8. I'm a believer in periodic performance reviews.
9. I retain receipts for all my purchases and expenses, even if they're not reimbursable.
10. I have a place at home where I feel comfortable doing career or personal paperwork.

Administrative Exercises

1. Develop a household budget that indicates how your current income is being spent.
2. Review your insurance policies (property, health, and life). Assess whether they meet your current needs, and make any necessary changes.
3. Make sure your important personal papers are well organized and safely stored.
4. Write a one-page paper evaluating current use of leisure time. List three areas for improvement.
5. Evaluate your current investments. Write a two-page strategic

planning paper on how your portfolio might change in the future to meet post-career needs.

6. Clean all unnecessary papers out of your desks at home and at your office.

7. Keep a written log of all your purchases for a two-week period.

A "Personal Project" for Skill Development

A self-designated personal project can help you exercise each of the seven retirement management skills. The project should be unconnected with your career, and should have a goal that's beyond mere maintenance or simply an odious task you've already been putting off. It should be something that leaves you feeling fulfilled. If you've been meaning to get the lawn resodded, by all means do it, but don't make this your project. A worthwhile personal project might be building a greenhouse in your backyard if you've always wanted an herb garden, or developing a hobby you've always been interested in. Each of the management skills will be put to use in turn to accomplish the project. Remember to use all seven of the skills to accomplish the goals at each step.

Step #1   Creativity

Use your imagination to make up a personal project that will require a degree of involvement you feel comfortable with and whose accomplishment will leave you feeling fulfilled. It may be a learning experience, a home improvement or development of a hobby.

Step #2   Analysis

Analyze the benefits of accomplishing your personal project, and the obstacles to bringing it to fruition.

Step #3   Communication

Discuss your personal project with your spouse or someone close to you whose opinion you trust. Solicit their input.

Step #4   Planning

Develop a workable plan for accomplishing your personal project.

Step #5   Flexibility
Develop three ways you could modify your plans for your personal project and still achieve the same goals.

Step #6   Implementation
Put the plans for your personal project into action. If you encounter difficulties, incorporate elements of your modified plans as necessary.

Step #7   Administration
Maintain oversight on your personal project. If you're having problems with it, write a status report assessing the stumbling blocks and develop a corrective strategy. Continue the oversight until the project is complete.

As you prepare for retirement, devote time to adapting these seven management skills to get a head start on achieving post-career goals. Plan on making retirement the next chapter in your success story.

Motivation in Retirement

Motivation and success go hand in hand. Executives exhibit a high level of motivation, which is stimulated by career-oriented influences. You'll have to supply your own motivatin in retirement, without reinforcement from your career. This can be one of the hardest tasks in adapting to retirement.

Consider these five Management Factors, the effect each has had on your career, and the comparable effect each now has on your "post-career" life:

Career & Post-career Management Factors

Career	MANAGEMENT FACTOR	Post-Career
Clear cut	GOALS	Amorphous
Externally generated	AGENDA	Internally generated
Visible	REWARDS & SUCCESS	Invisible
Competitive	PRESSURE	Non-Competitive
For Others	RESPONSIBILITY	For Oneself

P A R T II

THE CORPOREAL CORPORATION: FOUNDATION FOR A SUCCESSFUL RETIREMENT

The modern business organization is often portrayed as impersonal, but the reality is far different. Every business, large and small, develops a personality. It projects a sense of mission, an operating principle that identifies the company's character. This corporate personality is a function of the nature of the business, and the management philosophy behind the company. So we have buttoned-down, conservative financial service companies, old-fashioned, aging industrials, and young, freewheeling high-tech companies. There are stumbling giants and family businesses. Some are friendly, some aloof, others are ruthless. Corporate personality filters down and affects the way everyone in the organization views his job—bringing the staff together and, under ideal circumstances, creating a unified body, a corporate organism. The closer the company comes to being a fully integrated system, the healthier it is.

And so it is with an individual life. There's a personality, a harmony one can ideally orchestrate, and there's certainly business to be taken care of. There are sources of income, operating costs, resources to be maintained, plans of action to be effected. The product: a complete and successful life. The profit: fulfillment and enjoyment.

Imagine, for a moment, your future as an enterprise. What are your goals? Think of all the things you want to do, to learn, to see. Give your imagination and creativity freedom to roam.

Now imagine that you've been hired as the chief executive of this enterprise, charged with the responsibility of making sure these goals are realized. Suppose you've been given the job of running your life and achieving its objectives, and you have to report to a board that evaluates your performance. How would you manage your life? The most effective way would be to model your personal

64

enterprise along the same lines that have proven effective in your career, using management skills to define goals, set an agenda, and make sure things get done. This is the Corporeal Corporation.

The Corporeal Corporation is the vehicle for channeling your executive skills into post-career success. It's the blueprint for your future, your wholly-owned subsidiary. The Corporeal Corporation provides the framework for applying your management skills to retirement. It lets you view future goals, options, opportunities and problems in a business context, so you can apply your full range of executive know-how to getting the job done.

The Corporeal Corporation allows you to:

1. Translate vague post-career plans into definable goals.
2. Develop a workable agenda for achieving long-range objectives.
3. Package tasks and responsibilities in a way allowing sound management for optimum success.

As stressed in Part I, there are major differences between personal and business management. The bottom line is different. The competition is different. Nobody's trying to put you out of business or make a move on your position. The challenges are internal. The Corporeal Corporation will help you define the parameters of your post-career success, and keep you on the track to achieving it.

CHAPTER FIVE

CHOOSING
YOUR CORPOREAL
CORPORATION

Psychologists, consultants and management experts are finding new ways to unlock executive potential. In addition to studying case histories, deficit financing, and the nuts and bolts of business, today's executives packed off to executive seminars absorb many unbusinesslike lessons. Carnegie-Mellon University's senior executive seminar includes instruction in pottery and glassblowing. The Aspen Institute executive seminars include discussions of Plato and Dostoyevski. Outward Bound teaches executives teamwork by subjecting them to a rigorous week in the wilderness. At the Wharton Business School, executives undergo management training that includes this exercise: Imagine your company as a vehicle. Any kind of vehicle. Draw it on a piece of paper, and describe it in a few words. The exercise forces managers to view their companies as a whole, so they can set long-term goals and deploy resources to achieve them. The point of all this unorthodox instruction is to get managers thinking in new ways, to disrupt complacent attitudes of business-as-usual.

This same kind of new thinking is ideal to get you focused on your plans for the future, and help you define your post-career goals. Let's start by applying visualization techniques to defining your Corporeal Corporation, to identify what kind of "business" you want to be in. Imagine your future as a corporate entity. What kind of company is it? How could you maximize the effective operation of this company? To help, we list nine Corporeal Corporation models, based on the world of business. Most managers will be able to cast their future plans under one or more of these corporate banners.

Leisure and Entertainment Company

If you have diversified leisure interests, hobbies and an active social life, and favor them over a retirement that includes an ongoing business involvement, make the Leisure & Entertainment Company the model for your future. Plans that call for travel and living the good life can be adversely affected by attempts to keep one foot in the business world for appearances, or by your own ambivalence about a life of leisure.

One former corporate head found himself busier than ever in retirement. Sitting on boards, volunteer work and consulting filled his schedule; so much so that it interfered with the traveling and more relaxed living he and his wife had planned. To others it appeared that he had a healthy and balanced retirement, but he felt he had too many professional responsibilities to fulfill his goals. He gave up his directorships, and pursued the travel and social opportunities he'd been missing.

The Leisure & Entertainment Company requires solid capitalization and strict accounting practices. The potentially high expenses and costs of operation can put you out of business. Make sure you know how much of your assets can be channeled toward the expenses of non-recoupable goods and services.

Financial Institution

A background in business or finance can leave you with a large nest egg, and the acumen to manage it. The former president of an international bank occupies offices in the headquarters building; his company provides this perk to its top retired officers. From here he develops opportunities for venture capital investments and dabbles in other financial dealings. Any difference in his life since he retired? "Nope," he answers.

You don't have to be an international financial mogul to pattern your Corporeal Corporation on the Financial Institution model. Most of today's retiring professionals have considerable assets, and look forward to spending a little more time overseeing their stake and making it grow.

If you're going to take a more active hand in the stewardship of your resources, define part of the Corporeal Corporation as a Financial Institution. Subscribe to, read and clip financial publications. Get together with your broker and others who share your interests over drinks to talk investment ideas and speculate about market trends. If you're sufficiently skilled, consider offering seminars or other financial advisory services in a professional capacity.

Plan on charting a course of fiscal conservatism rather than taking bold risks which have the potential of greatly increasing or decreasing your net worth. This is particularly true for Reactive managers, who may try to find a substitute for their freewheeling executive style in the excitement of financial speculation.

R&D Firm

If you're considering a second career that would require additional training, or want to bolster current skills for the possibility of providing income or in pursuit of a serious hobby or interest, a Research and Development Firm can be your post-career corporate model. This will help you focus on the goals of your education, and keep you on the track of accomplishing them. These development efforts don't have to wait for the completion of your career before they commence.

Don't rule out "pure" research. Learning or educational experiences don't have to have income-producing potential to be worthy of your time and energy. And if you are working toward developing an employable skill, don't feel pressured to get a product—yourself—into the marketplace before it's ready; remember, this is an R&D Firm.

An advertising executive had a passion for American antiques, refined over years of hunting through flea markets and attending antique shows in the Northeast. To develop her interest in retirement, she planned a number of R&D efforts. She attended courses offered through a local university and a museum, and furthered her education by apprenticing herself to an antiques dealer. After two years and through contacts she developed, she could have started her own antique dealership, but after considering it decided to maintain the less demanding involvement she already had. She continues traipsing the circuit, her passion for antiques undiminished, and hires herself out as a consultant to collectors who appreciate her trained eye.

The High Tech Company

If you possess technical skills and/or knowledge in consistent demand, and want to use them in an ongoing professional capacity, cast your future in the mold of the High Tech Company. The goal: to maximize the activity-generating and profit-making potential of your specialized knowledge and skills. Executives are well aware of the volatility of the high-tech field. This applies to individuals, as well. Skills can quickly become obsolete, and the need for retraining and gaining knowledge of innovations is constant. At the other end of the spectrum, overspecialization can be equally problematic. Today's glamor industry can become tomorrow's corporate wasteland. Opportunities under this corporate banner can be elusive, but if realized, they can provide a high degree of fulfillment and financial return. Don't limit yourself to applying technical skills only as you did in your career.

A chemical industry executive began his career as a plant engineer. He enjoyed his management responsibilities as he worked his way up the ladder, but he missed the black and white problems of designing equipment or refining machinery. His vacation home was located in an affluent community with few service businesses. People's appliances were always breaking down, from pool pumps to balky VCRs. When he retired, he opened up a repair service that does a thriving year-round business. Though he's generally in town only during the winter months, he has a habit of showing up whenever he wants to do something with his hands.

The Consultancy

If you want to make use of management and business skills, either in a part-time capacity, or in an executive volunteer program, the Consultancy provides the business model. There are a wealth of opportunities for this Corporeal Corporation. Civic groups, charities, local governments, and nonprofit organizations are in desperate need of people with management know-how. This kind of post-career plan is ideal for those without consuming non-career interests, who want to stay involved in decision-making and give something back to society, without the pressure of a second career or solo business enterprise.

A former computer company executive found this model fit him perfectly when, during his transition period, he was tapped to serve on a Presidential task force on private sector initiative. He found the work extremely fulfilling, yet without the headaches of his job. His involvement pointed him in a positive post-career direction, and he hasn't looked back since.

It's important to identify both the management skills you have that can be applied in volunteer work, and the organizations where they can best be put to use. Organizations like the National Executive Service Corps, the Service Corps of Retired Executives, and the Fifty Plus Club can help.

The Mom and Pop Operation

Those who look forward to maintaining a very low-key retirement lifestyle, expanding activities they already enjoy instead of developing new ones, and making little outward change in their lives other than their reduced employment responsibilities, fall under the Mom and Pop Operation banner. These executives desire the simple pleasures close to home. This is an undemanding corporate model, and it can be difficult to adjust to for executives who led dynamic careers. If you've been a hard-charging professional, don't have many plans, and therefore see yourself in the Mom and Pop mold, be careful; you may be biting off much less than you bargained for. This shouldn't become your corporate model by default, because you can't think of anything better to do. It should be consciously selected by those who are looking for a simple lifestyle. The Mom and Pop style business is disappearing in corporate America, replaced by more aggressive organizations. But for those content with business-as-usual, the Mom and Pop operation can provide security and profitability without the headache of running a more high-powered concern.

Soon after college, a manager joined a small Midwestern equipment-leasing company. It began experiencing phenomenal growth, and his responsibilities grew along with it. He worked his way up to chief operating officer, in charge of a $350 million annual business, but always referred to himself as "just a country boy." As retirement approached and he planned his future, he realized he had few ambitions beyond having more time for his family, his hobbies and civic involvements. Because this model meshed with his desires and his management style, it was a success.

Real Estate Trust

Many executives plan on acquiring and developing a piece of property as a major part of their retirement plans. It may be a retirement home, a second home they want to spend more time in, or a farm they've always dreamed of owning. A number of retired oil executives have become cattle ranchers, which may reflect their knowledge of the business gained from investing in cattle-based tax shelters during their careers. Many of these retiree ranchers have managed to be successful in spite of the slump in the cattle industry as a whole.

If property, land or a home will play a big part in your retirement picture, consider the Real Estate Trust model. You'll need to devote time and resources to its maintenance, appreciation and enjoyment. The Real Estate Trust can be capital and labor intensive; substantial improvements in your facility may be required, but the potential profits of satisfaction, fulfillment, sense of ownership, and increased worth can be substantial.

Keep investment appreciation as a low priority goal. If you can't be satisfied with the intrinsic value of what you are investing your time and money in, you shouldn't be involved in a venture of this nature. If you want to make money in real estate, look into the R&D model for developing an educational plan to learn how.

The Conglomerate

Many executives maintain diversified interests in retirement. They may be engaged in activities that fit under the banner of several Corporeal Corporation models. These retirees are running a Conglomerate. Here, management responsibilities include overseeing several corporate identities, and ensuring that potentially disparate entities operate in harmony. They must know when it's time to abandon and/or sell off costly and unprofitable operations, despite emotional and personal attachments to them. A potential danger of any conglomerate is that so much time is spent overseeing the big picture that the individual components begin to suffer from neglect. In a matter of time, the entire organization shows signs of neglect.

An executive earned a good deal of renown putting together a business empire through shrewd acquisitions and tough deal-making. He collected companies like some men collect ties. He decided to retire, and sold off most of his holdings, moving into an aggressive post-career stance without batting an eye. He continued his globe-trotting and lavish lifestyle. He had homes in California, New York and Florida, and indulged his passion for art collecting and thoroughbred racing. He dabbled in real estate. But after a year of hopping from one residence to the next, he began to tire of his constant traveling. Formerly, he had frequently gone to the West Coast for business, but now he only went because he had a house there he felt he should take advantage of. He was overextending himself, not getting a sufficient return of satisfaction on his investment of time and energy. While he was attached to his California home, he sold it as soon as market conditions were favorable. He doesn't jump across the continent as much anymore, and rents a private home when business takes him to California. Meanwhile, he's finding his less hectic lifestyle is bringing him more satisfaction.

Which Corporeal Corporation is right for you? Don't expect to come up with an answer immediately. When corporations need to do strategic planning for the future, they dispatch executives to lavish rural retreats where they can ponder without the distractions of the office. Be prepared to apply this kind of leisurely decision-making to the issues of your future. Remember that your goals can change and evolve. The further you are from retirement, the more they're likely to change. But keeping these questions and issues in mind, and noting your changing desires, will help you make the right choices. Don't be constrained by the corporate models listed above. If none encompass what you have planned, develop your own.

Businesses diversify their interests, and so should you. We're not suggesting takeovers of unrelated businesses, mindless mergers or unjustified capital projects. Diversification of the Corporeal Corporation means expanding the possibilities and opportunities within the domain of your company. Whatever Corporeal Corporation you choose, and whatever activities and interests fall under its purview, look for ways to deploy your interests in new areas. Here are some examples: If you have an interest in hiking, start a program to take underprivileged youngsters on camping trips. Do you enjoy reading and literature? Enroll in literary criticism courses at a local university. An executive with a taste for fine food can start a gourmet club, with a monthly meal that members prepare at one of their homes. Use creativity to think of ways you can further expand, develop and diversify your interests.

CHAPTER SIX

TAKING INVENTORY

The choice of your Corporeal Corporation has to meet practical considerations. Do you have the resources to support your plans? Is your interest in travel strong enough to satisfy the requirements of a Leisure & Entertainment Company? Is your knowledge of computerized manufacturing deep enough to turn into a High-Tech Firm? What are your strengths and weaknesses, your profit centers and your low-margin areas? How will they affect your future? To get a handle on your assets and liabilities, you need to do what every business does—conduct an inventory.

To select the right Corporeal Corporation, five inventory areas of your life need to be examined. Each can strongly affect your future.

1. Relationships
2. Leisure and Social Activities
3. Health Status
4. Business/Employment Possibilities
5. Financial Situation

No matter what level of success you've reached in your profession, it's a new ballgame when retirement starts. Management skills remain, but the material you have to work with is different. The inventory covers the five areas that are the foundation for your future, and will indicate which are brick and which are straw.

The inventories are essential for realistic goal setting. They can save lots of self-delusion and misery, and help you to view the future realistically. If you're not sure what you want to do, these evaluations will help you decide, and objectively appraise your chances of success.

Each has an explanation of issues to keep in mind when conducting the inventory, followed by a self-evaluation worksheet. The evaluations aren't pass-fail tests. They don't have right or wrong answers, though some responses bode more positively than others. It's up to you to evaluate the results. Discuss the evaluations with others—family members, your company's personnel or human resources director, close friends, or others whose input you respect and know can be helpful.

Relationships

This is an assessment of your family ties, their role in your future, and the changes your retirement will have on these relationships. The relationships include:

- Spouse
- Children
- Parents
- Secondary family members

Family relationships play a vital role during the retirement transition and throughout the post-career years. A career has a powerful impact of its own on your relationships, and it's important to weigh the effect it has had. A successful career can add to an overall sense of well-being and contribute to a rewarding family life. Or the demands of a career can break up a marriage and splinter a family. A career can also be used to escape an already unhappy relationship, and be blamed for creating problems it only serves to shield you from.

It's imperative to consider how your career has affected your relationships, and look ahead to the changes retirement will bring. The interpersonal dynamics can change completely in your home.

RELATIONSHIP INVENTORY

1. List the family members with whom you live, or with whom you have regular contact.
2. Write a one-page paper describing each of these relationships.
3. Assess the impact your career has had on each of these relationships.
4. What effect do you anticipate retirement will have on these relationships.
5. How comfortable are you discussing personal and career problems with family members in this group?
6. If any of these relationships are currently problematic, what can be done to improve the situation? What are the chances of an improvement occurring?
7. How closely have you, or will you, discuss and agree upon post-career plans with your spouse?
8. Have you and your spouse made plans for independent activities, as well as joint ones, in the future?
9. List secondary relationships (in-laws, grandchildren, etc.) that you want to be part of your future. What do you expect from these relationships?
10. List your three biggest personal and career crises. How did each of your primary family members react to it?
11. If you have children, what changes in your relationship (financial, emotional) do you expect in the future?
12. If your or your spouse's parents are living, what changes in your relationship do you expect in the future?

Leisure and Social Activities

Leisure and social activities provide a major outlet for many retirees in their post-career years. For others, too many rounds of golf or cocktail parties can be a not-so-slow death. It's essential to know what part these activities play in your life, and how much you can depend on them for future fulfillment. Typical leisure and social activities include:

- Hobbies
- Learning Interests
- Vacations and Travel
- Friendships
- Civic Involvement
- Volunteer Work
- Club, Social Organization Membership

Leisure and social activities are major manifestations of personality. In leisure, one is free to pursue the interests that define the individual beyond the constraints of occupation. Socially, one is free to be with others of one's own choosing. While these relationships are without the depth of feeling of familial ties, they are also without the responsibilities. These activities are vital components of post-career life.

Post-career Leisure

Hobbies and fulfilling interests can bloom into consuming passions in retirement. On the other hand, if you get tense and jittery as soon as you leave the office, or never developed a range of non-career interests, you may need to compensate by planning for a second career, continuing employment, or emphasizing an involving volunteer commitment. Start planning now.

Vacations are an excellent indicator of your ability to detach yourself from your career. Being able to forget about the office for a couple of weeks, and enjoy travel, are big pluses in making the retirement transition. But if you always postpone vacations, claim you can't take the time off, or call the office everyday when you do tear yourself away, there could be trouble ahead.

Have realistic plans for adapting leisure activities to post-career demands. A corporate communications director with an avid interest in photography began with the simple step of having business cards made up with her name, phone number and the words "Professional Photographer" printed on it. She began getting weekend assignments, and took courses at the local university. Now she sells photos to magazines, her prints are shown in a gallery, and she has students of her own.

While having outside interests is important in adjusting to

retirement, so is avoiding the self-delusion of trying to transform an occasional interest into a full-time avocation or business. (We present specific strategies for trying out your interests prior to retirement in Chapters 4 and 5.) One executive loved the movies, but never got a chance to see as many as he wanted. Shortly before he retired, he got a VCR, and he and his wife started a list of all the movies that they wanted to rent. As a small retirement present, he bought himself a popcorn maker. He was going to have a ball! Three weeks and some 25 cassettes later, he didn't care if he never saw another movie in his life.

Some leisure activities aren't very expandable. Recognizing this avoids unrealistically relying on them for more fulfillment than they can deliver, which can create feelings of frustration and resentment.

Relearning to Play

Leisure activity is playtime. But many executives forget how to play. In getting ahead in their careers, the object is always winning, not the fun to be had along the way. Learning to enjoy an activity for itself, rather than as part of a win-lose reckoning, is an important part of the retirement transition. How much does the outcome matter to you compared to the enjoyment of the activity? When you play golf or tennis, how important is the score? Does the loser always buy the drinks? Too much emphasis on competition can take the fun out of leisure, but some managers may need to use competition in leisure activities to sublimate the competitive thirst formerly quenched by career. This need reaches its zenith in Overachiever personalities. Here competition in play can be put to good use.

Socializing After Your Career

We all need to interact with others. Socialization keeps us healthy and involved with the world. A strong social network helps you face the future without the feeling of going it alone. Yet your social ties will change considerably in post-career life. A large amount of the socialization need is derived through your career. Interactions with colleagues, business meetings and conventions, have strong social components. Consider how many of your friends are connected to your career, and gauge the impact your retirement will have on these relationships. Are you heavily involved in company events and activities (a Company Man characteristic)? Be prepared to consider substitute activities and friendships. Work-related social networks may keep you looking backward instead of forward. It's better to forge new associations reflecting a new lifestyle, and firmly send the message to yourself that a new beginning has taken place.

LEISURE AND SOCIAL INVENTORY

1. List your five favorite leisure and social activities in order of their importance to you.
2. How much time per month do you spend on these activities? How much additional time can these activities absorb and still be pleasurable?
3. Evaluate the satisfaction you derive from non-career time.
4. Evaluate the effect your career has on your leisure and social activities.
5. Write a list of activities that used to be hobbies in your life. Next to each, write a brief explanation of why you gave them up.
6. Write a list of leisure and social activities you don't have time for that you'd like to pursue in retirement.
7. List the friends you feel close to. Consider how retirement will affect your relationship with each.
8. List all social and civic organizations you are currently involved with. What impact will your retirement have on your involvement?
9. What groups and organizations would you like to be involved with that you're not currently?
10. Rate the importance of friendships and organizational involvements on your overall happiness.
11. Evaluate the vacations you've taken in the last five years. How well did you plan them? How fulfilling did you find them?

Health Inventory

The Health Inventory is an evaluation of your mental and physical vitality and resources, and their ability to withstand the challenges of the future. (For a more complete discussion of health, see Part IV: "Managing Your Health.") Your overall vitality has three components:

- Physical Health
- Mental Health
- Health Maintenance and Attitudes

It's hard to run a business if the physical plant is in danger of falling apart, constantly requires maintenance, or employees are subject to unsafe conditions. Similarly, without mental and physical health, it's impossible to run a successful retirement. Health problems divert time, attention, energy and finances from achieving long-term goals. Unhealthy attitudes can cloud decision-making as surely as poor physical health impedes operations.

Physical and mental health are linked, and the collapse of one can lead to a quick deterioration of the other. The emotional strain of retirement can be the trigger that sets off this chain reaction.

The healthy executive may underestimate the contribution of career to overall vitality. The purely physical demands of executive life require energy and stamina, and contribute to keeping one in shape; a career also adds tremendously to one's sense of emotional well-being. This vitality won't carry over into retirement automatically. You'll need programs to compensate. Golf twice a week isn't enough. Developing a sound and realistic program for post-career health requires motivation and effort. This inventory will help you see how involved you are in maintaining overall wellness now, and assist in developing a future health plan accordingly.

Companies have to respond to changes in the business environment. They may retool, abandon once-profitable operations, adapt to new methods and procedures to meet competitive challenges. Retirement can have a similar effect on an individual. Changing your standard operating procedure can be stressful and anxiety provoking. It takes strong emotional resources to meet the challenges. How well equipped are you? Your attitude about your career and the future, your management philosophy, how you've met adversity in the past, all provide clues revealing your emotional readiness and maturity.

You may note the professionalism with which you confronted potential emotional turmoil in the past—disagreements with colleagues, business setbacks, career disappointments—and be tempted to think this means you'll have no problem facing emotional challenges in the future. But the nature of business and the camaraderie of group challenge helps gloss over unsettling emotional issues, and provides a veneer of orderly professionalism that keeps executives on an even keel. In retirement the psyche is vulnerable to personal, rather than business emotional assault, and the isolation in which you face these challenges adds to the potential turmoil.

Your management personality says a lot about how you'll handle these challenges. Are you the type who always has to be "in control" (a strong Reactive tendency)? Without adjustment, your emotional framework may be too rigid to adapt to retirement, leaving you feeling lost, naked and defenseless. Executives who love playing the part of the hard-nosed businessman may consider exposing vulnerabilities a sign of weakness. In retirement, they may let problems consume them without trying to talk them over or seek help.

HEALTH INVENTORY

(The Health Inventory should be taken in conjunction with a complete physical examination.)

1. Describe your current physical health status.
2. List any past health problems and evaluate their chances of reoccurrence.
3. Consider the health status of your spouse, or other individual who will have a major role in your retirement.
4. Describe current health maintenance programs (exercise, special diets, check-ups, etc.).
5. Consider future programs that may be necessary to compensate for post-career lifestyle changes.
6. Describe your relationship with, and feelings about, your doctor.
7. List leisure activities you enjoy that involve physical activity.
8. List the five greatest emotional challenges of your adult life. Evaluate how you handled each.
9. Consider the importance of your career to your overall emotional well-being.
10. Compare your method of dealing with emotional issues in your career with your handling of non-career emotional issues.
11. How freely do you discuss troublesome issues with those close to you, or with impartial individuals?

12. Characterize your general mental attitude, your philosophy about life, and your feelings about your ability to influence your overall health.
13. What plans have you made to deal with the potential emotional trauma of retirement?

Business/Employment Possibilities

The Business/Employment Inventory examines your capacity and/or emotional need for income-producing activity in post-career life. The Inventory covers three areas:

- Marketable Skills
- Desire for Continued Employment
- Employment Opportunities Available

More executives are working past traditional retirement age, and there are more opportunities than ever to remain employed. But many executives who want or need (due to emotional reasons) to keep working haven't taken the time to adequately assess their options, or to develop a plan for marketing their skills.

If continued employment appeals to you, consider the reasons why. Being in touch with your motivation helps you make realistic decisions. Among the common reasons for continuing to work:

- Love of work
- Desire for new career challenge
- Boredom
- Lack of alternative activities
- Financial concerns (justified/unjustified)
- Inability to accept aging or retirement
- Avoidance of an unhappy home life
- Neurotic career fixation

Many executives who continue or return to work fall into the first two categories; they genuinely enjoy the ongoing challenge and involvement of employment. But look down the list and you'll see the other reasons are negative: an escape from something. Work as a refuge, a hiding place. Make sure a desire to keep working comes from positive rather than negative feelings. If you feel driven to work by a negative reason, it's much healthier to change your attitudes and behavior so you can experience new and challenging lifestyles.

If you want to start a business of your own, or convert a hobby into an income-producing activity, examine your reasons and objectively gauge your chances for success. Avoid a knee-jerk reaction to the question of continued employment arising out of fears about retirement.

BUSINESS/EMPLOYMENT INVENTORY

1. What is your attitude toward working beyond traditional retirement age?
2. What are the attitudes of close family members about your continued employment or retirement?
3. If you want to continue working, list the five main reasons why.
4. Develop a list of employment opportunities that would satisfy these needs.
5. List five good reasons for retiring.
6. What are the options of remaining in your present position in a full-time or part-time capacity beyond traditional retirement age?
7. Prepare a resume outlining your career history and work skills.
8. Prepare a list of any special employment skills you have.
9. List educational courses or executive training programs you've been involved in.
10. List the individuals in your career network who could help you in an employment search.
11. List headhunters, executive recruiters and employment counselors you would contact in a job search.
12. If you wish to start your own business, list 10 reasons why.
13. List 10 good reasons why you shouldn't start your own business.
14. How willing are you to take a lower-paying job, or a job in a different field, in order to remain employed?
15. How willing are you to retrain for a second career?

Financial Inventory

The Financial Inventory examines the effect of money on the retirement decision and post-career success. It includes these areas:

- Attitudes about Money
- Current Finances
- Spending Habits
- Projected Post-career Finances
- Post-career Capitalization Requirements

Money, and your attitudes about money, have a profound impact on retirement-related decisions, from when to retire, to your post-career lifestyle. Reaching financial goals is a major reason cited by executives and professionals for deciding when to retire. Freed of financial worries, future options expand enormously. Usually, money isn't the cause of post-career failure. But it's not unusual for unrealistic expectations or poor attitudes to have a negative impact. Most managers have the wherewithal to provide for themselves very comfortably. Unfortunately, poor financial management often makes this a moot possibility. Some overspend on grandiose post-career plans. Others, driven by unreasonable fears for future solvency, institute tightfisted budgeting practices and miss out on opportunities they could easily afford. A retired bank director living in Florida tells of the members of the local chapter of the Power Squadron, mostly wealthy retired executives, arguing about moving their weekly luncheon meetings to a better restaurant where the price of lunch would rise from $2.75 to $3.50 per person.

After a lifetime of equating pay with work, it's easy to develop phobias about not having enough money if we're not working. Financial fears have been exacerbated by the very real experiences of retirees who were subjected to the double digit inflation of the late 1970s and early '80s. Many retirees in all socioeconomic strata were forced to drastically alter their lifestyles, move to less costly housing, and curtail many of their favorite activities. The period of staggering inflation may be over, but the memory lingers.

Do some strategic planning. What will be the impact of the completion of your mortgage payments? How will financial obligations to your children change? Will aging parents of your own be depending on you for support?

It's vitally important to think about inflation, contingencies and possible financial calamities when projecting future financial needs, but don't let groundless fears and worries about money paralyze you. Focusing on your assets, liabilities and projected earnings and benefits can help you define your financial goals and devise realistic post-career budgeting.

FINANCIAL INVENTORY

(The Financial Inventory should be evaluated with input from corporate pension planners, accountants, financial planners, tax attorneys, estate planners and other financial experts.)

1. What part has financial planning played in your career goals?
2. Write down your financial goals. What part do they play in your retirement timetable?
3. Write down specific and vague financial worries you have about the future.
4. List current assets and liabilities.
5. How tightly is your income currently budgeted?
6. List major non-retirement financial changes you anticipate in the future, e.g., end of mortgage payments, college tuition payments, increased care of parents, inheritance.
7. Draw up a budget indicating the costs of your current lifestyle.
8. List the benefits you would receive at retirement for each year between the ages of 55 and 65.
9. Project your assets at the time of retirement. Include property, investments, benefits, insurance policies, Social Security, veterans benefits, IRAs, Keough Plans, savings, etc.
10. Estimate your annual income in retirement, basing your employment benefits on the age at which you're most likely to retire.
11. Forecast an annual budget for your planned post-career lifestyle. Take inflation into account.
12. Estimate your discretionary income in retirement.
13. Evaluate the ability of your finances to accommodate your post-career plans.

Inventory Evaluation

Don't try to complete the inventories in one sitting. The issues they raise should be thought about over time. Compare the results of each of the inventories with your plans as defined by the Corporeal Corporation. Do they fit? Are there problem areas? Can they be corrected? Match your hopes for the future with evidence of the past to select the right Corporeal Corporation, and recognize potential pitfalls on the path to achievement of your goals.

Most managers will be deficient in at least one inventory area. Strength in one may cause weakness in another. A passionate interest in flyfishing (Social and Leisure) may contribute to marital problems (Relationship). Opportunities indicated by a rich Business/Employment Inventory may have come at the expense of items in the Health Inventory, as a result of career-related or personality-generated pressure.

Any major decisions within the context of the Corporeal Corporation should be considered against the inventories. If you plan on relocating, but you've always been dependent on a strong social network, make sure you'll have substitute ones in place. Consider available social networks as part of your relocation decision.

Once you've defined your corporation, it's time to start thinking about how you're going to achieve the long-range goals of the company, pay the day-to-day operating expenses, and quickly and effectively get into the "business" you've chosen. You'll get more specific about your desires and objectives, and the ways you'll achieve them.

If your ideal Corporeal Corporation doesn't square with deficiencies in your inventory, don't assume you've made a mistake in setting your future course; you've found problem areas that require attention for your Corporeal Corporation to be a success. Make correcting problems or imbalances your first priorities for action, your first order of business. Begin working on them well before the retirement date. If you don't have enough leisure activities, begin developing them. Insufficient capital for your Real Estate Trust development fund? Set your financial targets now. Confronted with this corporate problem, you can turn your business savvy and know-how toward solving it.

The thoroughness of your plan will be partly influenced by your selection of "career." The Mom and Pop operation may not require a major business plan, if you've decided that's the most appropriate Corporeal Corporation. On the other hand, if you're considering a second career, under the R&D banner, using your skills for continued employment, particularly in starting a business of your own, your business plan must be very sophisticated.

Remember the importance of research. The greater the change from your present lifestyle, the more research and planning is needed.

CHAPTER SEVEN

CONSIDERING YOUR MANAGEMENT PERSONALITY

The problematic management personalities defined in Chapter Two can doom a Corporeal Corporation to failure if these behaviors aren't modified. Recognizing and accommodating these tendencies is a vital part of post-career planning.

The Reactive Manager

Reactives poorly handle more sendentary retirement lifestyles, or ones that revolve around rarely varying schedules. They can compensate by maintaining dynamic components in their life, from continued employment to intense involvement in a non-career interest, or civic involvement. It's important to make sure the Reactive tendencies mesh with these new involvements. One Reactive retiree had to be "fired" from an executive volunteer group; he couldn't accept his advisory capacity, and continually demanded the organizations he was ostensibly helping do things his way.

Avoid Seat-of-the-pants Management

Inadequate planning is a hallmark of Reactive personalities. Instead of thinking things through, they prefer to respond to developments as they arise. In work, conditions constantly change without input. In retirement, without input and planning, things stagnate. Devote time to developing a positive post-career agenda.

Avoid Overly Grandiose Plans

When they do plan, Reactive managers are prone to make ambitious plans that require excessive levels of performance. Their pride is at stake, and they refuse to seek help or alter unrealistic goals. The more ambitious their plans, the more important it is to make sure they're completely prepared. Thoroughly discussing plans with others can provide valuable feedback that helps ensure their objectives are realistic.

Pay Attention to Financial Management

Reactive managers can get in over their heads if they forget they're dealing with a personal, not a corporate budget. They need to pay close attention to finances, and concentrate on steering a course of financial conservatism, avoiding "hot tips" and wild investment schemes that appeal to their sensibilities.

The Overachiever

Like Reactives, sedentary post-career lifestyles or low-keyed leisure agendas aren't advisable for Overachievers. Achievement orientation needs to be refocused on challenges of the future. For those who don't want to enter a second career or continue employment, developing new skills or seriously pursuing an interest can provide enough involvement and competitive challenge to accommodate these tendencies. Activities should involve others whom the Overachiever can "compete" against, from sports, to fund-raising for volunteer groups, where achievements are measurable.

Stimulate Post-Career Competition
Discuss informal plans for the future with others in similar positions. This leads to benevolent competition as you strive to outperform others in implementing your plans. Build specific targets of accomplishment into your plans, to create yardsticks of achievement. Make goals quantifiable; enroll in at least one educational class, reduce weight (if necessary) two pounds per month, etc.

Avoid Excessive Competition
Don't set your goals too high, a classic Overachiever behavior. Even if they're achievable, goals set too high can take the fun out of reaching them, and create unnecessary pressure. When articulating your agenda, phrase it by saying, "I want to achieve . . ." a certain objective, not "I must" or "I have to."

Monitor Competitive Drive
The Overachiever must remain aware of how the competitive drive affects his activities. Otherwise, his competitive urge may be indulged at the expense of achieving more long-range objectives. If competitive drives are channeled into planning ahead, the Overachiever has an excellent chance of developing a comprehensive and thorough agenda, and enjoying substantial post-career success.

The Company Man

Once they overcome excessive career dependence, this category's executives have a variety of fulfilling post-career agendas they can be successful in. In general, they don't need to compensate for the same intense and dynamic drives possessed by Reactive and Overachiever personalities. If they seek continued employment, it can be simple part-time involvement supplementing a varied and undemanding schedule. They can be comfortable in the traditional model of a leisurely retirement.

Adjust Career Identification
Close identification with career and company needs to be either compensated for or accommodated. Social and leisure interests are

often overly career-dependent—friends from work and company-sponsored social events are very important to company men. But without the common bond of career, these ties loosen, and shared activities with career-connected friends become less rewarding. There are two ways to handle this problem. Through compensation, an intensive effort to develop extra-career interests and ties helps the executive define himself outside of career, as he creates a support network and interests that will sustain him in the future. Through accommodation, executives can investigate possibilities for ongoing inclusion in company activities and social events. More companies are making efforts to retain ties with former employees, providing them with the opportunity for part-time or temporary work, and establishing social organizations for their retirees, allowing for continued participation in company-sponsored activities.

Challenge Yourself
The Company Man often relies on an externally imposed agenda. Without this outside input of assigned tasks, he may fall into a rut of dull routine, or settle into a stable but unfulfilling lifestyle. The Company Man has to challenge himself, and examine whether he's getting as much as he wants out of his life. Otherwise, abilities may lie dormant, and opportunities go unrealized.

The Combat Vet

If the Vet can recapture the dynamism of his early career, the sky's the limit for the future. The first task is to consider whether there's another problematic management personality masked by his current situation. If so, it needs to be taken into account, so that he doesn't trade in one set of counterproductive behaviors for another.

Start Small
Since the Vet can be so beaten down he feels it's fruitless to try orchestrating his future, the key is to take small steps to reassert himself and provide positive reinforcement. Involvement in a class or part-time employment that will make him a vital part of an organized group is an excellent way to accomplish this. The resulting rediscovered self-confidence will carry over into other aspects of his post-career life, allowing him to take a dynamic view of the future.

Ready for the Future

We've defined the theoretical underpinnings of executive retirement management: the executive personalities, the changing world of retirement, the adaptation of management skills to the challenges of the future, and the modeling of post-career lifestyles. With these principles in mind, you're ready to start the hands-on work of the retirement transition in the office and at home.

P A R T III

THE RETIREMENT
TRANSITION

Let's get down to the business of putting retirement management principles to work. The mechanics of your retirement transition in the career environment will depend on three variables:

1. The size of your company
2. Your company's retirement programs and policies
3. Your position in the company

Whether or not there's an ideal retirement transition, there's certainly no typical one. Each organization has different attitudes and practices regarding retirement, and each executive reacts in a unique way to the organizational and emotional issues involved, producing an infinite number of transition scenarios.

Starting the Transition

The most common question executives have about the retirement transition: "When should it start?" The answer: Earlier is better. Some planners advise starting to plan your first day on the job. In reality, few of us are so perspicacious. Don't feel you've missed the boat if you're in the middle of your career and haven't done any solid planning yet. Executives who entered the workforce a decade or more ago weren't encouraged to do the thorough kind of retirement planning as today's young execs are. While it's never too late to start planning, it's never too early, either. Sometime between now and the end of your career you need to become familiar with a host of retirement issues. Get moving now if you haven't already.

Here's a general timetable for retirement planning. Obviously some executives will have an accelerated schedule, leaving their careers well before 60.

A Retirement Planning Timetable

Age	Planning Activity
30-40	Define career goals.
	Examine annual benefits statements.
	Develop meaningful leisure activities.
	Think about second career if present one is unsatisfying.
40-50	Promote career independence.
	Learn company early retirement policy.
	Discuss post-career issues and goals with spouse or other close individual.
50-60	Begin serious retirement preparation in all areas.
	Develop all-star team of advisors.
	Review career.
	Estimate or set retirement date.
60-70	Set retirement date.
	Oversee executive succession.
	Retire, implement post-career plans.

Make sure you've covered all the steps not only for your current age, but also for the ages before it as well. Why do executives avoid this kind of preparation? There are many reasons. We talked about some of them in Chapter 1. There are others, too; almost none are rational.

Five Fallacies of Retirement Planning

1. Planning for retirement is the kiss of career death.
2. By focusing on the future, planning for retirement shortchanges the organization.
3. If I plan for retirement, it will precipitate the arrival of retirement.
4. Retirement planning is an indication of job dissatisfaction.
5. Preparing for retirement will make me feel old, and lead others to think I'm older than I am.

Any fallacy or subconscious fear that leads you to postpone preparation is harmful to you and your organization, because retirement planning is important for both.

Pretirement—The Big Picture

View the total transitional program under the banner of "Pretirement." Pretirement is all the steps and exercises you undertake to get on the road to your post-career future. It's a "big picture" concept that brings the four transitional stages—realization, acceptance, disengagement, separation—together and makes them a unified whole. While there are specific issues to deal with and objectives to accomplish in each state of the retirement transition, you may be more comfortable now focusing on them as part of one agenda.

Incorporating

Setting an agenda for your future involves the following three components:

1. Choosing Your Corporeal Corporation
2. Taking Inventory
3. Considering Your Management Personality

Thinking about these elements individually, and the way each affects the others, will bring you to a healthy and realistic view of your future. Now it's time to formalize the planning process. Serious business proposals, contracts and other vital communications are always put in writing. Your future deserves the same attention.

- *Define your Corporeal Corporation.* State the type, and expand upon it by explaining your objectives as specifically and concisely as possible.
- *Set an agenda.* Draw up a list of the things you need to do now to set your plans in motion. Establish your projected date of retirement, and what needs to be accomplished by then. Outline your plans for your first year of post-career life.
- *List the major problems.* you foresee in reaching your objectives, and how you plan to overcome them.
- *Sign the document.* This seals your agreement to work toward the goals you've set for yourself.
- *Review the plans.* At least once a year examine these letters of incorporation to check your progress and institute any necessary changes in plans or objectives.

CHAPTER EIGHT

THE RETIREMENT TRANSITION IN THE OFFICE

Companies realize handsome dividends when executives effectively plan for retirement. Senior executives have the most experience and responsibility. Yet as they approach the apex of their careers, retirement fears come to the fore: "What will I do with my time?" "Does this mean I'm washed up?" "It's all downhill anyway, so what's the use of putting out on the job?" Negative thoughts have a devastating impact on performance.

Executives who plan for retirement, who know where they stand, and have a rational view of the future, are more valuable in their most productive years than executives wracked with doubt or undergoing emotional crises.

There's another way companies profit from a clear and supportive policy toward maturing executives. Many executives hide their retirement plans from their companies because they are unsure of how the company will react, particularly if they are considering early retirement. Unfortunately, this is a fear that is sometimes well-grounded, as in the extreme case of one manager who announced to the company president he planned to take early retirement in 10 years—and was fired on the spot!

The result: Many executives keep their planned retirement date to themselves for as long as possible. They rob themselves of the opportunity to plan openly for retirement, and the company misses the chance for an effective and thorough management succession. Companies with enlightened retirement policies and effective retirement planning programs don't face this problem.

Realization

Realization takes place primarily in the executive's mind. As stated in Chapter 1, the goal of Realization is simple: to convince you that retirement is more than an abstract concept. Once you've grasped that retirement is really going to occur, you will be galvanized to prepare for it.

Prior to Realization, managers typically define long-range goals in career terms: a target salary figure, a position they hope to hold in the future. Once Realization occurs, the horizon of your long-term plans will expand to include post-career goals.

Objectives:

- Accept the reality of retirement.
- Stimulate thoughts about the future.
- Consider career goals vs. life goals.

GETTING ORGANIZED

Calendars, memos and diaries are an everyday part of executive life. They help you keep track of schedules, things that need doing, thoughts on projects already underway. The phenomenal popularity of executive "day planners" and similar comprehensive appointment books indicates recognition of the importance of personal organization. Apply this principle to your retirement transition. This is an important project, and deserves and needs its own paperwork. Acquire a log book, notebooks and other office supplies for keeping track of the business of your retirement. Write down pertinent information and insights about your transition and post-career future. Use the notebooks for any transitional exercises that require writing, and date all the entries.

Start a "future file" (more about this in Chapter 9). Clip articles and save documents pertaining to your outside interests or future plans. This kind of organization is a great way to get you thinking about the future at any time in your career. You can fill up several memo books by the time you're ready to retire. Looking back through these records can be an invaluable reminder of the work you've done to prepare, giving you added confidence about your ability to meet upcoming challenges in retirement.

CAREER GOALS VS. LIFE GOALS

When considering the future, think about two sets of goals: career goals and life goals. Too many execs think they're the same. If you confuse what you want from your career with what you want from life, retirement will be a flop whether you achieve your career goals or not.

Determining what you want out of these two areas of life isn't always easy. The decision making provokes the same questions that have haunted philosophers for centuries: What's life all about? Why am I here? What is worth striving for in life?

These questions have no right and wrong answers. Everyone must decide for themselves. Getting help isn't cheating. Involve family members, particularly your spouse, when you wrestle with these issues. Anyone strongly affected by the decisions you reach should be consulted.

To help you focus, take a sheet of paper from your future file. Head one side of the paper, "Career Goals." Head the other side, "Life Goals." Here are some general ideas of what people want. Make your list as specific as possible.

Career Goals

Attaining a top position
Reaching financial targets
A satisfying career
Influence over policy
Making a contribution to society
Recognition for accomplishments

Life Goals

Raising a family
A desirable lifestyle
Rewarding marriage
Respect in the community
Pursuit of personal interests
Maintaining health

Focus on your non-career goals of today, and project them into the future in five-year intervals. How are they likely to change? What ways are there for you to measure progress? How do life goals mesh with your career goals?

These two sets of goals are often in conflict. The demands of achieving career goals can stand in the way of realizing personal ones. A few years ago, executives were more willing to put personal goals behind them to get where they wanted in their careers, but we are now seeing healthy changes. Executives are seeking more balance in their lives, and companies are getting a little suspicious of single-minded managers willing to give up everything to get ahead. Fewer relocate for their jobs, formerly a *de rigueur* sacrifice for career advancement. A recent survey found more executives who said they were reluctant or unwilling to relocate for their careers than said they were willing to move.

If you have a good idea about your life goals, and find they're inconsistent with career goals, start bringing the two into line. Getting your goals working together can create hardship and disruption, but the longer you put it off, the harder and more disruptive it is. An executive in his early fifties who aspired to become company president, but didn't want to retire at age 62 as his company's mandatory retirement policy for senior executives dictated, took a job with a smaller firm where he could work as long as he wanted. Another top executive felt his career was taking too much away from his family, and scaled back his work schedule, though he knew it could hurt his career. He was comfortable with his choice, became more effective in his work, and, three years later was promoted to president.

Don't be discouraged if you have difficulty defining life goals, or if they're in conflict with career goals. Discovering what you really want out of life can take time, but you can speed up the process by making a conscious effort at self-discovery. Creativity and Analysis are key retirement management skills that will help you. Let your imagination open up various future scenarios for your career and life, so you can choose the path that suits you best.

Keep in mind your projected date of retirement. If it's still 20 years away, uncertainty about career and life goals is understandable. If it's 10 years away or less, accelerate efforts to define your goals if you're not sure of them already.

Analyzing what you like and don't like about your job can help you focus on activities and plans for the future. What are the most fulfilling things in your career? Look back over your scheduling book. What are the tasks that you spend most time on? Which are the things you enjoy most? Incorporate aspects of these tasks into your future plans. One hard-driving CEO wondered which of the many offers of directorships, consulting contracts, volunteer services, and other feelers he'd received he should pursue. Thinking about his present work, he realized one of his favorite aspects of the job was the time spent at 35,000 feet in the company jet, where he could read and relax in peace and solitude. As a result of his insight, he made sure his post-career workload left ample time for less hectic pursuits.

As your transition proceeds, periodically review the Career/Life Goals chart, to see if your goals have changed, and if not, check on your progress in achieving them.

LIFE GOALS PLANNING EXERCISES

1. Imagine a "perfect week" that doesn't include work. Where would you spend this week? What would you do? What activities would you be involved in? What kind of food would you eat? What people would you want spending it with you?
2. Consider the perfect week you just imagined. Is this a lifestyle you'd be comfortable maintaining over a long period of time, or a special week you think you'd soon grow tired of or be exhausted by?
3. Imagine a perfect year. How does it differ from your perfect week? What elements of your perfect week or year are currently in your life? How could you incorporate more of them?
4. What were some of the first things you dreamed of being when you grew up? Cowboy, fireman, doctor, nurse? What made you choose those roles, and why did you change your mind about them?
5. Pretend someone close to you asks for career guidance. What would you tell them are the most important things they should keep in mind when selecting a career or particular job?
6. Imagine you could alter your past. What would you change about it, and why?

YOUR ORGANIZATION'S PROFILE

The size and structure of your company, and where you fit into it, plays a role in post-career planning. How large is the company you work for? How many layers of management? The bigger the company, the more layers, the greater the need to downshift to reorient yourself to the future.

The senior manager of a large corporation has a two-fold problem. First, he's grown accustomed to a great deal of power and the satisfaction of people reporting to him. Second, he may be removed from the hands on, day-to-day aspect of his business, concentrating on planning, strategy and delegation instead. Subordinates won't be available to carry out directives in retirement.

With a bit of work, you can overcome this reliance. Make yourself try different things, handle some simple tasks, even if they don't seem very appealing on the surface. If you haven't typed a letter in years, type one now. If someone else puts calls through for you, do it yourself on specified days. The same with screening your calls. You'll be surprised at the power of these minor tasks in helping reorient you to your future. The discontinuity between career and post-career life won't seem so abrupt.

There's a silver lining in this insulated cloud top managers are accustomed to. Executives of large companies have an easier time finding post-career work as consultants or partners in smaller companies. They've usually built up a larger network of contacts who can help them find these opportunities, and the classic management training they've received in their careers can be applied to virtually any organization.

REALIZATION EXERCISES

1. Estimate when you'll retire.
2. Establish career, life and financial goals.
3. Attend a company retirement party.
4. Drop by the office of an executive in your organization who's about to retire.
5. Examine company benefits statements.
6. Learn the details of your company's retirement policy.
7. Have a lighthearted discussion of post-career plans and fantasies with some colleagues.
8. Discuss your employment experiences to date with a close friend or colleague.
9. Chat with a subordinate whose current position corresponds to your first job with present or former employer.
10. Take a personal day off from work and enjoy yourself.

Acceptance

The final decade of a career will begin the hands-on work of Pretirement—this includes formalizing post-career plans, attending retirement seminars, experimenting with post-career lifestyles, and later, downshifting emotional and management involvement. Acceptance is the first part of this hands-on transition. It's the stage of dealing with unwarranted fears and doubts and moving past them. In the office environment, you take more active steps to plan for the future, and gather more information in preparation for it. However, you won't downgrade career involvement during Acceptance. You'll find that realistically addressing the emotional issues of retirement and refining post-career plans will add to your management capabilities.

There's a lot to accomplish. Acceptance coincides with the executive's peak career years. You're making lots of money. There are major projects you're responsible for. Career-wise, you're more involved than ever—and you have to start getting ready to leave the poker game, take your money and go home. It's also a time to review your career. Have you gotten where you want to go? If not, can you get there? How can you best cap your career?

Meanwhile, you've grown attached to the perquisites of your career. A company credit card feeds and entertains you. A company limo picks you up. You play golf at the country club at which your company has thoughtfully provided you with membership. At tax time, company financial planners help with your finances. And one day, when you're dining on that credit card, or riding in the limo, or playing golf, you are going to wonder how you can give it up. By taking a hands-on approach to the future during Acceptance, you'll gain the confidence and develop the enthusiasm to overcome your negative emotions.

Objectives:
- Deal with emotional issues of retirement.
- Articulate post-career plans.
- Commence concrete retirement planning.

THE RETIREMENT DECISION

The date and timing of retirement is one of the most important decisions of the retirement transition—not *the* most, but one of them. During Realization you thought about your retirement date in a general way. Now, during Acceptance, your plans become more concrete. The answer will be affected by many variables. Company policy, your own desires, and events in the work environment can all play a role.

Does your company enforce mandatory retirement for executives at your level, or the level you expect to be at? While mandatory retirement as a matter of written policy usually applies only to the most rarefied levels of the management these days, a corporate culture often sends an unspoken edict to maturing executives to vacate their positions. Learn all you can about your company's policies and your options. Even in companies with mandatory retirement for top positions, a senior executive could trade down his job, and continue working in a lesser capacity. Few of these executives do, but don't limit your options to those defined by common practice.

If mandatory retirement, either written or unwritten, is non-existent or irrelevant in your case, there are other factors to keep in mind. Don't think of retirement as an arbitrary age or date. In many cases, it's helpful to consider your role in the organization, and target a retirement date that fits in with this larger picture.

- If you're overseeing a project. Completion of a major project is often a good time to peg your retirement date to. The satisfaction of achievement leaves you feeling you're going out like a winner.
- If your company has periodic reorganizations. Large companies that undergo regularly scheduled management reorganizations may provide you with the right opportunity for bowing out. The restructuring may come every three or four years, and be time-consuming and involving. There's little sense in enduring this kind of reorganization if you don't plan to stick around until the next one.
- When successors are ready. If you've made your intentions about retiring known, without fixing a date, you're probably overseeing the transfer of your responsibilities to another executive, or their absorption into other departments. When you've passed the reins, it's a good time to say goodbye.

Unspoken policies and attitudes are important to be aware of when considering when to retire. Some companies don't involve executives over 55 or 60 as much in important projects, and reduce their responsibilities. Some executives appreciate the chance to decelerate gradually from their careers, but others take the "play me or trade me" attitude. Knowing your attitude and your company's unwritten policies will help you plan accordingly.

Executives who need to get an idea of when to retire in more general terms should examine the career and life goals they've defined for themselves. When career goals have been met—or when you've reached a point where your life goals are achievable, even if your career goals aren't—is a good time to retire. By the age of 50 you'll know if you're on track with your career goals. If you're not, it may be time to switch priorities in your life goals, and consider the possibility of an early retirement.

A survey of over 1,000 executives, published by the American Management Associations, found the following issues were either "important" or "very important" in setting their retirement age:

Financial concerns	94%
Desire for more family ties	83%
Desire to pursue personal interests	81%
Company policy	79%
Desire for a second career	40%
Desire to start a small business	30%

As you can see, this survey didn't ask about health status as a factor in retirement, but don't downplay the significance of your health in the retirement decision. The life of the modern executive is somewhere between demanding and punishing. If you feel you've pushed yourself as far as you care to, it's time to get out.

Your own feelings about when to retire are very likely to change over the course of your career. In the survey above, the older the executives responding, the more likely they were to desire time for personal interests, and the more willing to scale back career responsibilities to pursue them.

THE PERSONNEL OFFICE

Your company's headquarters for information about benefits, pension, and company-sponsored retirement planning can play a vital role in the retirement transition. It goes by a variety of names: the human resources department, the benefits planning office, the industrial relations office or the personnel office. In some companies it may be under the direction of the medical department or even the recreation department. In small businesses, an executive may deal with an office manager who wears many hats, and retirement advice may not be his forte. No matter what your company calls it, who's running it, and how much they know about post-career planning, your objectives are the same in every case:

- Broaching the subject of retirement in an official capacity.
- Learning about available retirement planning and assistance programs.
- Getting retirement financial information.

Broaching the Subject

Realization was largely a one-person mental exercise. You thought about career and life goals, made efforts to reconcile them, and courted the reality of retirement. Sitting down with whoever handles retirement issues at your company puts your retirement plans into an active mode. It sends a clear message to yourself that you're starting the hands-on work of retirement planning. And it starts filling in the blanks, answering the questions you've had about pragmatic retirement issues.

One manager who hadn't yet hit 50 had to battle a very strong urge to resist this step. "I was worried people would think I'd been approached about a new job, and was comparing benefits before I decided."

Today's corporate personnel and human resources officers are delighted when executives take the initiative to inquire about retirement issues, instead of having to be dragged kicking and screaming into consultations. Give them a call, and arrange a mutually convenient time to meet. This is itself one of the best Acceptance exercises you can undertake.

Learning about Programs

Planning for the future is primarily your job, but it never hurts to have help. More companies are assisting the transition with a tremendous diversity of seminars, workshops and one-on-one counseling. Some smaller companies participate in "consortium" programs, where several businesses jointly sponsor retirement training programs through community colleges or other educational institutions. Knowing what you can expect from your company will help you in planning and feeling in control of your future. Knowing what to expect will also help you compensate for company programs that are deficient in key areas. (See Appendix A.)

Getting Financial Information

If you've been doing your planning right so far, you've got ideas about your future lifestyle and the cost of maintaining it. You have financial goals. You've also been keeping tabs on your annual benefits statement, noting the contributions and performance of your pension plan to date, and projections on what your retirement benefits will be at different ages. But accumulating benefits and annual statements tell only part of the story. You need the complete picture of your retirement benefits and other retirement financial matters. Company officials can provide it. They can also give you a much clearer idea of your benefits package once you're ready to discuss retirement dates. (See Appendix B.)

Redefining Yourself

Finding an identity outside of your career is one of the most important tasks of Acceptance. Focus on the many non-career roles you already play—parent, spouse, golfer, tennis bum, part-time handyman, movie buff, gourmet chef.

1. Write a three-page on who you are, without referring to your career.
2. Think of an older relative you felt close to who had a career, and how you defined him through your relationship.
3. Think about the relationships you have with people who don't know you through your career (neighbor, social organization members, store clerk). Focus on three of these individuals, and write a half-page paper on each of them imagining how they define you.

Any steps you take to think about the future are excellent Realization and Acceptance exercises. Reading this book, or any guide to retirement or post-career life and planning qualifies. Making the effort to deal with retirement issues shows an intelligent and mature perspective. Those who resist, or figure they don't need to prepare, are most at risk, and should be the first to plunge into transition exercises.

ACCEPTANCE EXERCISES

1. Write down your planned date of retirement.
2. List the changes and prepatory steps necessary in your career to accomodate your post-career plans.
3. Think about your future with the company, and assess how high you're likely to advance on the career ladder.
4. Call three retired executives you know and say hello.
5. List the five things you most enjoy about your career, and the five things you like the least.
6. Start a "future file" of news clippings and other information for post-career planning and action.
7. Buy a copy of a magazine with a 55+ demographic.
8. Talk to a retired relative (father if possible) about his experiences on reaching retirement age.
9. Get information from the personnel department about benefits and training programs.
10. Re-evaluate your career goals/life goals chart.

Disengagement

Disengagement signals the active downshifting of career and the acceleration of implementing a personal agenda.

Objectives:

- Reduce emotional involvement.
- Reduce career commitment.
- Assist in management transition.
- Participate in formal retirement training programs, if not done yet.
- Complete personal projects.
- Experiment with post-career lifestyle.
- Complete post-career planning.
- Handle the long goodbye.

REDUCING CAREER COMMITMENT AND EMOTIONAL IN-VOLVEMENT

Some managers carry an emotional involvement with their company far into retirement. They maintain ties, attend corporate retiree groups, and cling to their former corporate identity. This is fine, as long as the manager realizes the need for the prolonged involvement and that opportunities for ongoing corporate involvement exist. But for the manager who wants to forge a new life and tackle new challenges, the emotional disengagement from career is much more important. Physically reducing the time you spend overseeing operations is an excellent way to downshift emotionally. Scaling down obligations is beneficial for you and your company, and it's something a growing number of organizations recognize. More companies are instituting formal succession programs for top executives that incorporate a gradual handing over of responsibilities to their designated successors.

This process should begin from three to five years before the expected date of retirement. To get a handle on reducing management obligations start by defining your anticipated responsibilities over the remainder of your career.

1. List all projects you're currently involved in.
2. List projects you expect to be involved in initiating or overseeing.
3. Evaluate successor candidates.

Consider your personal stake in projects you're involved in. Are these pet projects you've been pushing for a long time, that were initiated at your insistence? Are they projects you've only grudgingly agreed are necessary? Your attitude toward these projects can help you get a fix on your emotional involvement with them. Identify which are vanity projects (yours or someone else's), and which ones are vital to the company. Pull the plug on your vanity projects as expeditiously as possible. Someone else's that you are incapable of stopping should be turned over to a subordinate. The necessary projects are the ones that will really test your emotional disengagement. Gradually reduce "hands on" involvement, turning it over to someone in contention to succeed you. Set up a reporting mechanism that will keep you appraised of progress, but limit your input as much as possible. Take pride in how well you've trained the individual who has taken on the task.

When you initiate or are part of new projects during disengagement, keep your involvement in a "coach" capacity, remaining on the sidelines and watching the action on the field, making sure it's running according to your game plan.

The selection of your successor is an important part of Disengagement. Your company policy and your position in the organization determine the amount of input you'll have in this decision. Having the opportunity to help select and prepare your successor helps you feel a sense of continuity, of not leaving loose ends. Make a list of the requirements of your position, and the qualifications a successor would ideally possess. Identify individuals (a maximum of three) in your organization who are appropriate candidates. Evaluate each—state what they need to learn, and how much seasoning they require. Update your evaluation annually. If you are asked for input on your successor, you'll have this information ready, and can begin the training as required. If you don't have any input, you'll most likely be asked to assist in training the replacement who's been selected; the notes you've made will help you zero in on the skills and knowledge your successor needs, and what you will need to teach him. This creates a positive feeling of continuity almost as much as if you'd hand-selected the successor yourself.

In selecting a successor, two sets of needs come into play—yours and the company's. Managers seek their own form of immortality through those who take over for them. The want to see their way of doing things, their philosophy, carried on; it's a tremendous affirmation of the job they've been doing. Unfortunately, this isn't always either wise or called for, and it's imperative to understand that operational changes are sometimes necessary. When the tight-lipped and bookish CEO of a major computer company was succeeded by an outgoing, high-profile executive, company insiders said it was a conscious and needed change—not because of any deficiencies of the departed CEO, but because the changing business environment required more of a figurehead who could be a commanding spokesman for the organization and the industry.

Not all executives take these changes in procedure in stride. The ex-head of a sales organization was livid when his successor altered the forms and paperwork requirements he'd developed, and he began calling his former sales reps in the field to complain about the changes.

If you have a voice in tapping your successor, avoid the temptation to judge contenders by the way you would have done things. Take into account changing times and business conditions. Continued success can usually be achieved with a different management style, and indeed is sometimes required by it. Have a frank discussion with top executives about their perceptions of evolving company needs, and whether your departure is looked upon as a time to start making some changes. Without this dialogue, you may make improper succession decisions, and interpret any subsequent changes as meaning, "we couldn't wait to see you go."

In many organizations, the successor decision is made approximately six months before the date of retirement. It's kept confidential among those making the decision, the prospective retiree and his replacement. The retiring executive is asked to work more closely with his successor and prepare him for the new responsibilities. A formal announcement on the selection is made several weeks prior to the manager's retirement.

Being shut out of the successor decision can generate negative feelings, but that perception can change. As one former executive said, "I felt left out at the time, but what if the person I chose didn't work out? Now I'm glad I didn't have any input."

Even with proper planning, whether you have a say in your successor or not, the passing of power can be far from smooth. Nature abhors a vacuum, and many corporate execs feel just as strongly about the power vacuum your departure can create. Your position may become a prime focus of political maneuvering. The choice of your successor can be greatly influenced by internal politics, and it's easy to get caught up in it. You may be thrust into an emotionally wrenching experience at a time when you should be reducing emotional involvement in career. In the extreme, this last bitter struggle can wipe out memories of decades of achievement, and lead to a brooding aftermath that can dominate the former executive's life.

RETIREMENT REHEARSAL

Some companies are giving executives a chance to "test the waters" of retirement through rehearsal programs. These go by such names as "tapering off," "phased retirement" and "retirement rehearsal." The thoroughness of these corporate programs varies. Some take the form of work schedules that are gradually reduced to three days a week over the last three or five years of employment, others offer three- to six-month sabbaticals. If the executive finds the non-working life isn't for him, he can come back to work full time. (In virtually all of these programs, pay is reduced commensurate with the reduced workload.)

Chance are your company doesn't have a program like this; only around 1% of companies do, according to recent surveys. If this is the case, investigate the possibility of designing your own rehearsal or making yourself a guinea pig for a program like this, if the concept appeals to you and it's feasible for your organization. Talk to those with the authority to give you the go-ahead, and be ready to work out details to make sure your responsibilities will be adequately handled.

Some programs begin with a simple reduction in the number of hours spent on the job per week—say, from 40 to 30 or 35 hours. For them to be effective, though, you need to reduce the number of days you work, not the number of hours. Using the extra time to come in a little late every day, or leave a little early, won't help. Even if the work week is only reduced five hours, work four nine-hour days, not five seven-hour days. You need full days to put your post-career plans into practice.

First and foremost is the importance of having plans to test. Don't plunge into a rehearsal program hoping to discover what you want to do—the objective is to test plans you've already made. You should already have developed a prototype Corporeal Corporation (see Part II), and be using this time to start up operations.

The amount of time away from your career should increase the closer you get to retirement. Ideally, during the last one year to six months of your career you should be spending only three days at the office, with the other two being spent on experimenting with your post-career plans. The emphasis is on the word "experimenting." One executive had plans to go after his Ph.D. in history, and spent his self-designed rehearsal investigating programs at nearby universities, talking to professors, and refining his ideas about the period of European history he wanted to study. The more he investigated, the less he felt he wanted or needed to get the degree. He decided he'd be much happier just taking a few courses he was interested in, and dispensing with the sheepskin he'd thought he wanted. By investigating first, he was able to make definitive plans based on good research.

Experimenting while you're still working takes away lots of the pressure you feel about finding a new identity for yourself when your career is over.

CAREER REVIEW

One of the most important Disengagement exercises from a psychological standpoint is the career review. The review helps you distance yourself from your career by taking a big step back to look at it, examine the high points and the low points, consider what you wanted out of it, and what you got. If you don't come to grips with the meaning and purpose of your career, and what your accomplishments and failings have been, a sense of unfinished business can follow you into retirement.

Answer the following questions in writing:

1. What were your long-range goals at the beginning of your career?
2. How have your goals changed over the course of your career?
3. How successful were you in achieving your goals.?
4. What are the major factors that prevented you or assisted you in reaching your goals?
5. What were the five high points in your career?
6. What were your five greatest career disappointments?
7. What individual stamps, such as new procedures instituted, new areas of business, etc., have you left on companies you've worked for?
8. Write a three-page strategic paper on changes in your department, division or company that you feel will be necessary in your company's future.

THE RETIREMENT MEMO

How will people know you're going to retire? Nobody wants to fade away or become a non-person overnight. Companies have several mechanisms to spread the word for you. The posted memo is one common method. Announcements in the company newspaper are another. Local newspapers may also be alerted.

If there's anything special you'd like mentioned in the announcement, make your wishes known to the officer who handles this responsibility. You may plan to move to another city. Including that in the announcement may pave the way for new social contacts. You'd be surprised at how far and fast news like this can travel.

THE RETIREMENT CELEBRATION

Let's take an elevator up about a hundred miles and do some aerial anthropology. Look at that ceremony on the plains of the Serengeti in Africa. That elderly Maasai is giving up his spear. The ritual signifies he's moving from being a warrior to a tribal sage. And look there, in the heart of the United States, in that banquet hall. The man now stepping up to the lectern is a top executive, giving a formal farewell to his colleagues at a retirement dinner.

Retirement dinners, testimonials and parties are rife with symbolism. They serve the emotional needs of those you leave behind as much as they serve yours, and perhaps more. Co-workers have to come to terms with your impending absence, and the need can be quite strong, depending on your relationship with colleagues and subordinates, and the impact you've had on the company. Even those you're not close to feel the hands of time when they see you depart. But while everyone has emotional needs, keep yours first. Discuss what kind of send-off you'll be given, and take a part in planning the kind of gathering you'll be comfortable with.

Until recently, retirement parties were often handled insensitively. The gifts ranged from clocks and watches with their constant reminder of passing time, to rocking chairs. The retiring president of a department store chain was given a beautiful engraved clock—with his name spelled wrong on it! "If that's what happens to the boss, I wonder how other people cope with being shunted aside," he remembers thinking. Thankfully, most retirement celebrations today are done more tastefully.

The retirement fete doesn't have to be the traditional testimonial or last-day-at-the-office party. The divisional president of a clothing manufacturer dreaded the thought of a testimonial, especially after all the dreary ones he'd attended. He put the word out well in advance, and a year before he retired he was the guest of honor at a dinner announcing the most profitable year in the division's history. It was understood by all present that it was a tribute to his career which would soon be ending, and it fulfilled the emotional need to say farewell without the baggage or heaviness of a retirement dinner right before departure.

The three founders of a major advertising agency were approaching retirement. One was in poor health, and there was a feeling a retirement party would degenerate into a sad and wistful affair. Instead they threw a lavish 20th anniversary party for the agency aboard a boat. The three thanked everyone for making the agency grow, and sent a clear message that they'd soon be turning over the reins.

In virtually all companies, a retirement gathering of some sort is held. The kind of occasion, and the guest list, vary considerably. Some large companies honor everyone who's retiring that month. Some invite everyone in the company, others restrict guests to those in a department, or give the retiring executive an opportunity to draw up the guest list. Do you have to have a retirement party if you don't want one? No. However, making a fuss over refusing this kind of gathering may indicate an improper retirement acceptance. If you don't want to have a party, make sure it's not because you can't face retirement. There are other alternatives, some of which you should take advantage of even if you are planning a more formal occasion; gatherings over drinks and other get-togethers with closer associates shortly before retirement give you and your colleagues an opportunity to let your hair down and talk about old times in a less buttoned-down setting.

CLEANING OUT YOUR OFFICE

Cleaning out your office can be a melancholy job. There are ways to reduce the impact. Start removing a few non-essential things several weeks beforehand. It's a good way to help disengage yourself from your career, and prevents the air of finality that accompanies a massive, one-day office clean-out. Also, find out about the disposition of papers, documents and files well before the last day. Which will the company need, and which will be disposed of? Will files be transferred to another office? Making plans beforehand saves a last-minute rush through an important part of the retirement transition. When you begin the final cleanout, involve a subordinate or colleague you feel close to whose tenure is approximately equal to yours. It helps sharing the memories these papers evoke with someone who can appreciate them, who's been there with you.

Save personal papers that have meaning to you, but avoid shipping boxes of useless correspondence and memos to your home, where one of two things will happen to them: They'll sit gathering dust, or you'll go through them from time to time, continuing to dwell on the past when you should be concerned about the future. If you can't face throwing things out yourself, turn material over to the appropriate company officers, and let them worry about it. Better yet, throw them out yourself. These papers and documents played a part in your career, but don't feel bad about not needing them for the next chapter of your success story.

Some companies allow executives to return after retirement to handle the final steps of vacating their office. If your company has no specified policy, think about which schedule you'll be most comfortable with, and settle on a timetable with the appropriate company officers in advance.

Make it a point to learn company protocol for handling other rites of retirement. In larger companies there's usually a standard procedure and a checklist for turning in company credit cards, photo I.D.s, company car, and other instruments of your office. Debriefing is often involved, as well. If you've been working with proprietary information, there'll probably be a discussion of what you're allowed to divulge if you seek similar employment. You may be asked to sign an agreement spelling out these constraints.

Allow sufficient time for tying up these last loose ends of your career. Things get hectic as retirement approaches, and it's important to leave without feeling rushed in the final transition from the office to retirement.

THE LAST DAY

How is the final day of work selected? Sometimes it's dictated by company policy, sometimes it's a decision the retiree is free to make on his own. When company policy is involved, the final day of a calendar month may be the retirement date, for bookkeeping purposes. If the 31st is a Wednesday, you won't show up on Thursday. If it falls on a weekend, the Friday before will be the last day. If you have vacation time coming, you can usually apply this towards the retirement date, and, for instance, take your last "vacation" two weeks before retirement, and not come back.

If you're selecting the date yourself, consider what will make you most comfortable. Friday seems like a natural, but some executives might find the first Monday of retirement a bit jarring after completing a normal workweek. When questioned about selecting a final day, one executive, himself head of a retirement counseling service said, "I never thought about it before, but now that you ask, I think I'll make it a Monday. They're usually so slow. That'll put some excitement into it."

KEEPING IN TOUCH

Many executives plan on keeping in touch with former colleagues after retirement. Be realistic about these plans. Perhaps being a shade pessimistic is appropriate. Ties with colleagues loosen dramatically after retirement. Those higher up in the management ranks are frequently discouraged from keeping in regular contact for fear it will be perceived as meddling. Additionally, many at the top of the corporate totem pole may find those they perceived as friends were only interested in them because of their titles. As the former president of a large retail merchandising company said, "This reality of relationships, while easy to understand intellectually, is unpleasant to accept emotionally."

Be aware of these realities, but don't let them stop you attempting to retain some contact with associates. Formalize vague plans to keep in touch. Make an index card or create a database on each business associate you want to stay in contact with. Along with their address and phone number, list how often you expect to see them, and what you'll do. It doesn't have to be anything more ambitious than lunch. On the card or on the computer, track your contacts with each person. Once every two or three months is plenty of contact to start with. Keeping data like this will encourage you to develop more social contacts. With this mechanism in place to track social contacts, you're more likely to pursue them.

DISENGAGEMENT EXERCISES

1. Pick one afternoon to be out of the office for three weeks in a row. (The same day each week.)
2. Move a prize memento from your office to your home.
3. At the next appropriate social gathering, make it a point not to discuss business or your career.
4. Write an imaginary testimonial speech on what your career has meant to you.

5. Write down your three biggest career successes, your three biggest disappointments.
6. Begin going through your papers and office files with a long-time colleague in attendance.
7. Select a suitable project you would normally handle. Turn it over to a trusted subordinate. (Ask for progress reports.)
8. Attend a meeting of a retired executives' group.
9. Meet with an independent financial planner to assess your financial situation.
10. Complete and test plans for your Corporeal Corporation.

You're now ready to face the future head on. Don't be alarmed by the butterflies in your stomach—they're normal. Don't try to minimize the challenges ahead—they are as substantial as they seem. But don't sell yourself short on your ability to meet them.

When you began your career, the challenges you faced were even greater. You were untested, and you had to compete every day with other dedicated and motivated people. Now you've concluded a successful career. You've proven you've got what it takes. From here on out, the only person who can keep you from being successful is you.

CHAPTER NINE

THE RETIREMENT TRANSITION AT HOME

Half of the stress of retirement comes from leaving your career. The other half is from coming home. Unfortunately, many executives think the retirement transition at home starts after the last day of work. That's one reason many of them botch the job. Prepare for retirement at home as soon as you start preparing for it in the office. At work, you reduce emotional commitment and involvement, in effect, extricating yourself from your career. At home, commitment and involvement increase, and you become more integrated. Even a second career, or other lifestyle that keeps you away from your home, requires an at-home retirement transition. Retirement creates a changing dynamic that affects all those around you, no matter what form retirement takes. The changes must be recognized and accommodated.

All four phases of the retirement transition have a place at home. Realization, Acceptance and Disengagement have in-house agendas corresponding to those handled in the office. Separation, the final stage of the transition, takes place entirely at home after

121

your career. Indeed, while thoughts of retirement typically center on career, even greater attention needs to be placed on what's going to happen at home. This is the arena in which your retirement management skills will be put to the ultimate test.

Realization

Realization fosters an awareness of your retirement—and retirement issues—to those close to you. It's about opening up channels of communication, and developing a group front for facing the future.

At the point of career in which Realization optimally occurs (10 to 15 years before retirement), commitment to work frequently contributes to tension in the home environment. Dedication to career and the consequent diminishing of family life can create feelings of neglect and resentment. Discussing Realization issues helps both you and those close to you put your career in perspective. It becomes less threatening, and indeed becomes the road to long-term happiness and fulfillment.

Objectives:

- Stimulate spouse/family to consider the future.
- Encourage recognition of need for in-home transition.
- Foster view of career as part of longer-range goals.

MANAGING EMOTIONS IN THE HOME

Effective managers don't allow subjectivity to interfere with decision making and implementation. In your career, you deal with hard-headed superiors and stubborn subordinates on a professional level, without emotions getting in the way. Major problems await the executive who attempts to transfer this style of hands-off emotional management to the home.

The Five Rules of Constructive Emotional Management at Home:

1. Be aware of the power and the glory of subjective feelings.
2. Be honest with yourself and those close to you about your feelings.

3. Openly discuss the way you feel and things that bother you.
4. Be willing to compromise.
5. Remember there's often no right or wrong in dealing with emotions.

In the business world, you deal in facts. In the home, you deal with feelings. Here, subjectivity reigns supreme. You're dealing with close personal relationships, not colleagues bound by professional commitment. "People problems" arise, but they need different solutions from those at work; and you're no longer the cool, dispassionate executive observing the problem and attempting to apply answers from the outside. You're smack in the middle of any conflict—indeed, you may be the cause of it!

Retirement management isn't a matter of sweeping feelings aside while you develop flowcharts for household chores, or circulate memos for family members to initial. Try this heavy-handed home management approach and you're likely to have a strike on your hands. Dealing with emotions is a vital part of retirement, and it's one of the hardest lessons for executives to learn.

Not all executives take a hands-off approach to emotions during career. Think about your relationships with colleagues and subordinates at work. Psychologists and management experts are discovering these relationships may mirror those found in a family. Does this apply to you? Do you think of yourself as a father figure to subordinates. A stingy uncle doling out meager amounts of praise? A benevolent grandfather who hates to be the disciplinarian? Some familial patterns expressed in your career may be appropriate in the home. Examine the behavior you demonstrate in your career, and consider which characteristics may have a place in your future. Retain the best elements of this behavior, and get rid of the worst.

By training, managers play it close to the vest. They encourage others to talk while they listen. They keep emotions in check. Retrain yourself to be more emotionally active. If you have trouble opening up, start by talking about small things. Comment on how pretty the sky looks today. Complain that you're getting bored with your favorite breakfast cereal, and that you're going to force yourself to try some new ones. Discuss an issue on the editorial page that affects you.

More Emotional Management Rules to Keep in Mind

1. If nothing bothers you about your retirement transition, or leaves you feeling confused about the future, you're highly unusual.

2. Don't expect to find all the answers to handling emotional problems in a management handbook.
3. Solutions must be personalized. What works in your household won't necessarily work in another.
4. Use communication skills to discuss problem areas and illuminate feelings.

RETIREMENT—THE FAMILY CONNECTION

When contemplating retirement from within your career, it's easy to become preoccupied with self. You think of the changes overtaking you, your years of hard work, sacrifices you've made. Now comes retirement, a production you're going to direct and star in. How can you help but become self-centered, even if it is years away?

Anytime you start feeling like you're at the center of the universe, remember you're not the only one who's profoundly affected by your retirement. Your spouse, family or others you are closely involved with will play a key role in the success or failure of your transition into retirement.

But this family connection goes beyond enlisting their support for the changes you're going through. The fact is, your retirement means a major change for them, too, and this altered family and household dynamic needs to be recognized and accommodated.

Basically, two major aspects of the home dynamic change in retirement:

1. Time
2. Roles

Time
Even the most family-oriented executive doesn't spend much time at home. Marriage is a five-hour-a-day proposition. Even evenings and weekends, when the executive is physically home, he may be wrapped up mentally in work he's brought from the office. Retirement will drastically alter the amount and the type of time spent at home. The downside of this is summed up in the cliche, "I married him for better or worse, but not for lunch." The reality of this extra time, and how it's going to be spent, is an issue to start thinking about during Realization. Of course, it's possible that you'll

find it's like your honeymoon all over again, as you bask in the glow of each other's company, but be forewarned that this is rarely the case. Couples who haven't prepared, especially if the recent retiree doesn't know what to do with himself, are quickly at each other's throats.

Roles

Retirement represents a time of changing roles for you, your spouse and children; and this requires adjustment.

Retirement can create the same feeling of aging and uncertainty in executives' spouses as it does in executives. They see themselves as retiring, too. For spouses of high-level executives, career identification can be as strong as it is for the executive. They often define themselves through their spouses' careers, and relinquishing the role of the executive spouse can be difficult. One female retirement advisor specializes in counseling the wives of retiring senior executives as part of company-sponsored retirement seminars. "They often have a harder time adjusting to retirement than their husbands do," she says. "They miss the perks and the status."

Consider the profile of your homelife and marital relationship when thinking about in-home role adaptation. Who's is charge of what around the house? If your spouse is the de facto household manager now, this is an area of potential role confusion in the future. Newfound interest in household operations you've ignored for years may be resented. You're invading someone else's turf. It's vital to discuss and plan for these changes well in advance.

Even in two-career couples, the male executive has typically relinquished the major share of day-to-day household operations to his wife. Her outside interests, be it a full-time career, part-time work or volunteer activities, won't diminish her sense of territory in the home. In this situation, it's imperative to address not only the changing home dynamic, but also your spouse's outside commitments and their impact on your retirement. You may be ready to pull up stakes and move into a leisure lifestyle, but your spouse may not want to stop working. Only through open discussion can you develop mutually agreeable plans. Be prepared to compromise. Remember, *flexibility* is one of the key management skills of retirement.

As an executive, you can gradually adjust to impending retirement in your career, reducing emotional involvement and perhaps reducing time commitments. Make sure you and your spouse put as much effort into adjusting to the changes retirement will bring to your home.

Relationships with children also change during the retirement transition. Your retirement becomes a concrete marker of their own growth. Most children react positively to the question of retirement. They tend to view the parent-executive as having worked very hard, and as deserving a less pressured existence. They are supportive, but often have an overly optimistic view of retirement, and take financial security and satisfactory emotional adjustments as a given. The transition usually occurs as children reach adulthood. Don't be surprised if they begin treating you in a paternalistic manner. They view retirement in the traditional and somewhat outdated way: a time to take it easy, a signal of declining capabilities. For an executive accustomed to being the undenied head of family and head of household, this evolving relationship may trigger subconscious Oedipal fears. Potentially harmless jokes about being "over the hill" may hit home with a lot more impact than intended. "They made me feel like I was ready for a rest home," is how one executive put it.

Not all executives are married and have families, but all need some external support mechanism to assist with their adjustment to retirement. Close friends and blood relatives can fill the bill. Relations with these people can change just as do those with family members. Whether you have a family or not, it's important to maintain and strengthen a retirement support network, and to consider the impact of retirement on relationships with those closest to you.

LAYING THE GROUNDWORK

There are more than family issues to begin thinking about during Realization. Are plans and goals you're formulating workable and realistic under present circumstances, or will they require substantial adjustment? What about your housing needs in the future? There are legal and administrative matters to consider, like updating insurance policies and your changing tax situation.

Your home will be the headquarters for examining non-career

issues. Begin your transition as far in advance as possible, refining and adjusting your plans the closer you get to retirement. Your involvement over time in these efforts not only makes your transition and retirement easier, but also pays dividends in terms of a more rewarding home life long before your career ends.

REALIZATION EXERCISES FOR THE HOME

1. Have a discussion with your spouse about both sets of your parents. What kind of life are they leading? Did they plan sufficiently? What did they do right? What did they do wrong? What can you learn from them?
2. Discuss your overall career plans with your spouse.
3. Go through home photo albums with your spouse, or screen home movies that show both of you and/or your children at a younger age.
4. Have a general discussion with your children about their career plans.
5. Admire a beautiful sunset, and realize the sun is still shining over the horizon.

Acceptance

In the office, Acceptance is a mental exercise. It's dealt with during the executive's most productive years, and no effort is made to reduce career involvement. However, in the home environment Acceptance should include more active steps to prepare you and your family for the changes post-career life will bring.

Look back over the Relationship Inventory in Chapter 6 with your spouse. This inventory will give you an indication of how things stack up on the home front. When you've completed it, and noted areas that need improvement, draw up a plan of action for correcting problem areas. Plan on periodic reviews of the inventories to chart your progress in correcting deficiencies and updating other factors.

In general, children don't have to be included in the formal inventory evaluation process, but don't hesitate to solicit their input, or take them into account. One couple was reluctant to plan a move to Florida, worrying that their children, one living on her own in the same city, and another away at college, would feel abandoned. After discussing the move with them, they received their children's blessings, and worked out a plan for frequent visits.

The inventory may reveal legitimate problem areas in various relationships. Start dealing with them now. A remarried executive nearing retirement was concerned about his relationship with his young stepson. He knew that when he retired the youngster would only be in his early teens, and felt there would be problems ahead without more active efforts to improve the relationship. Discussing the situation with his wife, they planned activities that would include just the executive and his stepson, giving them a chance to establish a stronger relationship. This also helped his relationship with his wife, who'd been worried her son was missing an active father figure.

Acceptance is the time for you and your spouse to assess your mutual life goals. You may have a perfect idea of what you want to do with your future, but if these objectives aren't shared by your partner, your enterprise is doomed from the start.

Objectives:

- Involve spouse/family members in planning for future.
- Establish consensus on future goals.
- Identify problem areas for correction.
- Focus on necessary in-home adaptation.

THE HOME OFFICE

You probably already have desk space at home you use for work and personal business. Plan on upgrading the space. The home office is beneficial for two reasons:

1. You'll need increased office space for your personal management responsibilities.
2. Expanding office space at home helps compensate for the impending loss of office space at work.

Establishing or expanding a home office is an excellent transition exercise. You're going to need adequate space for record keeping, administration and correspondence. You're also going to need space you can call your own. One executive had an addition built onto his house for an office in anticipation of retirement. Three days a week he's in his office by 9:30, takes a break for lunch, and goes back to the home office until 5 p.m. to handle personal business.

Buying a new desk or file cabinets can help build enthusiasm for getting your office enhancement started. We touched upon the "Future File" during the previous chapter on the office transition, but the home is where you really make this concept work for you. Start clipping newspaper and magazine articles about subjects that interest you, or activities you might like to pursue in the future. Create a filing and storage system that keeps this data accessible. (Your future file won't do much good if all your clippings wind up buried in a huge box where they're difficult to get to.) Keep a record of the subjects of all the articles you save. Examine the list periodically, and see if it gives you any hints of associated areas of interest you could pursue. Also, examine the list to make sure you're taking positive steps to do something to develop these interests, and not just collecting articles about them.

Get an address file, and start putting in addresses and phone numbers of organizations or other groups that are involved in any interests of yours. Develop a library of information and source books concerning areas of interest you intend to focus on in the future. Have personal stationery printed up. This at-home headquarters will ease your transition from career to post-career life and help you maintain a sense of identity.

Keep a schedule book, memos to remind yourself of things to do, and a planning sheet for long-range projects, with a timetable for completion and periodic reviews. Maintain a set of transitional exercise notebooks for the home, just as you established at the office. Using these organizational mechanisms associated with the office in your home can be a very helpful transitional aid.

YOUR BOARD OF ADVISORS

During Acceptance as you solidify your future plans, define the Corporeal Corporation(s) under which they fall. Use the model to state objectives and set procedures for attaining them. Running a corporation isn't a one-, or even two-person job. Even the most self-assured CEO doesn't do it alone. He has a board of advisors and directors to help. So should you. Develop an all-star team of experts for your board, who you'll be able to turn to for legal, financial, emotional and whatever other kind of advice you may need. Among other categories of expert advice you may require: real estate, medical, insurance, and estate planning. Solicit help from experts in the area you've selected as the basis for your Corporeal Corporation, as well as for input on hobbies and other activities. Planning on doing woodworking in the garage? Locate a local craftsman who can share knowledge on technique, sources of raw materials, and other pertinent information. If you're modeling yourself as a Leisure and Entertainment Company and plan to do lots of traveling, get to know travel agents, or the editors of travel magazines, and develop a relationship that will give you access to their expertise.

DEVELOPING LEISURE ACTIVITIES

Acceptance is the time to start developing as well as defining post-career plans. Leisure activities take on major importance during the post-career years, and it's important to appraise their strength beforehand. Keep the following two facts in mind:

1. Rewarding interests and rich social ties can provide the fulfillment currently derived from career.
2. Unrealistic expectations about the depth of your interests or strength of social ties can leave you feeling betrayed, empty, depressed and without direction.

Fully evaluating extra-career interests before you retire avoids unpleasant surprises and starts you on the road to developing meaningful activities (if you don't have any already). Look back at the Leisure & Social Inventory from Chapter 6, to see how you stack up in this department.

Executives generally fall into three camps regarding extra-career interests:

1. Those with current outside interests.
2. Those without current outside interests, but with plans for pursuing interests in the future.
3. Those without current outside interests, and without plans for pursuing interests in the future.

Executives with Current Outside Interests

It's not the quantity of your outside interests, but the quality that counts. A laundry list of extra-career activities says little in itself. One executive had only one major non-career interest: sailing. Not much chance for indulging in this passion very often, you say? The last few years of his career he spent hand-building a 52-foot sailboat in his backyard with the help of his family. By the time he retired, he was ready to launch it in Boston harbor; and his hobby has given a center to his life ever since. Another executive had a smorgasbord of extra-career interests: hunting, trips to Vegas and Atlantic City, skiing in Gstaad. But after retirement he found none provided the fulfillment he got from his career. Following therapy, he sought part-time consulting work to provide him with a feeling of self his hobbies didn't provide.

Test out your hobbies and social plans to see if they're as stimulating as you think. Using the diversification principle, start fully developing your hobby and spin-off interests. Put creativity to work. If you like stamp collecting, visit local dealers and discuss your collection. Drop in on a meeting of the local philatelic society. Buy books on the subject, meet other collectors. Arrange a tour of a large regional post office. Apply the same approach to all the activities you hope to pursue in retirement. If you're a tennis bum, concentrate on your game. Investigate advanced lessons, learn about tournaments for your age bracket, visit and play as many area courts and clubs as possible. Ditto with painting, golf, anything.

Try immersing yourself in each of your activities and hobbies. The immersion test gives a clear idea of how deeply your interest goes, and what role the activity will play in your future. If you find your interest in stamp collecting is no more than an every-other-weekend hobby, fine. Don't give it up. But don't delude yourself into thinking it's going to become a major focus of your life, either.

Executives without Current Outside Interests, but with Plans for Pursuing Interests in the Future

A significant group of executives haven't developed meaningful leisure interests, but are brimming with ideas about what they plan to do once they have the time. If you fit into this category, start by listing your planned activities under one of these four headings:

1.   Hobbies I will develop.
2.   Leisure activities I will engage in.

3.   Social activities I will engage in.
4.   Civic organizations and volunteer groups I will join.

Now that the list is staring you in the face, start doing something about it. Begin sampling the activities you've listed. If you've always thought bowling was fascinating, spend an evening or two at the lanes. If you suspect the great outdoors is your thing, arrange to go on a day hike with a local nature group. Interested in making your community an even better place? Survey the organizations, civic groups or political clubs whose interests coincide with yours.

Take your time with this agenda. Rushing through these activities, from one to the next, won't give you a clear idea of your real potential interest in any of them. If you have a long list, it could take a couple of years to leisurely sample all the activities. When you've finished, you'll probably have discovered some activities you find very stimulating, some you find mildly interesting, and some that bore you. Now you're at the same stage as those who've always had extra-career interests. Try developing your more serious interests through diversification as suggested for the previous group of executives.

Executives without Current Outside Interests, and without Plans for Pursuing Interests in the Future

Some executives have few or no current outside interests, and draw a blank when asked how they plan to fill their post-career time. The first step for them is to come up with a list of potential interests similar to the list developed by executives in the previous example.

Activity Development Exercises

1.   List every hobby you had as a youngster.
2.   List all clubs you belonged to in school.
3.   Do you prefer being indoors or outdoors?
4.   What are the five most enjoyable things you've done in your life?
5.   List every job you fantasized having as a youngster.
6.   What are your favorite kinds of movies and TV shows?
7.   Do you prefer working by yourself or with others?
8.   If you had to choose a small store to browse through for two hours, what kind of store would it be?
9.   Do you consider yourself more of an artist or a technician?
10. What are the five achievements you're most proud of in your life?
11. Do you prefer projects with a clearly defined beginning and end, or ones that are ongoing?

Still drawing a blank? Talk to your spouse about activities he or she thinks you might enjoy. What activities does your spouse enjoy that you might try? What activities are friends of yours engaged in? Go along while they pursue their interests. See if you get any ideas from them. Once you've developed a list of possible post-career interests, develop a sampling program like the one outlined above, and then proceed to the diversification test.

If you still can't find any outside interests? There are some executives who are wrapped up in their careers to the exclusion of everything else, who may never develop rewarding outside interests. The operative word here is rewarding. There's no sense in doing something solely for the sake of keeping busy. If nothing outside of your career holds any interest for you, take a long look at your Business/Employment Inventory. You're a candidate for continued employment, and you should concentrate on developing skills and contacts that will allow you to keep working.

ACTIVITY DEVELOPMENT FUND

No matter what your level of outside interests, one way to assure you maximize your opportunities in taking advantage of them is to build an activity development fund into your budget. This is money you allocate annually for leisure or leisure development. You can spend it on a monthly basis, or save it up to spend on a big-ticket item. The important thing is to make sure you spend it, whether it goes to books, a pair of hip-wading boots, or art lessons. Building this into your budget will force you to involve yourself in leisure activities you might otherwise pass up. It was only after he budgeted $1,000 a year for a development fund that a former bank vice president got involved with pottery and ceramics. After taking lessons, he increased his budget, and now has a home studio with a pottery wheel and small kiln. It's strictly a hobby, but one that he greatly enjoys, and that he never would have taken up if it weren't for the activity development fund.

TO MOVE OR NOT TO MOVE

Housing is one of the most important post-career decisions. Allot ample time to think about whether you want to stay put or move, and where you might move to. Start addressing these questions during Acceptance. Whether you live in the city or country, chances are your present housing is determined by five primary factors:

1. Design amenities of house and property
2. Convenience to place of work
3. Necessary size to accommodate family
4. Convenience to schools
5. Desirability of neighborhood

Several of these factors may become moot points in retirement. You don't need to commute to work. Children may be ready to leave the nest, or already have, obviating the need for a large home and proximity to schools. Neighborhood desirability is still a factor, but there are desirable neighborhoods all over the country, and the nature of what you consider "desirable" can change considerably during post-career life.

The first step in getting a handle on post-career housing is to evaluate your present home. With your spouse, divide a sheet of paper in half lengthwise. Label the top of one side "Benefits of Current Home," and the other, "Drawbacks of Current Home." Don't restrict your thinking to your house in particular. Consider the neighborhood, region of the country and climate. Some of the common benefits and drawbacks are in the following table:

Benefits of Current Home	Drawbacks of Current Home
Finally have decorating scheme the way we want it.	House is too big for expected needs.
Friends live nearby.	Maintenance costs are high.
Very good neighborhood.	Don't like the climate.
Convenient to leisure activities.	House needs major improvements.
House is paid for.	Don't socialize with neighbors.
Property value is rising.	Enjoyable leisure activities are far away.
Plenty of room.	Property values are stagnant or beginning to decline.
Low property taxes.	Area has become overcrowded.
Very used to current home.	

Be as specific as possible with these two lists. If you ultimately decide to move, the lists will help you identify key items to either look for or avoid in a new community and house. If you decide to stay, you'll see the problem areas that can be changed so you can enjoy your home all the more. These two lists are often in conflict, presenting compelling reasons to both stay and go. That's why it's important to provide ample time to think about this. Your home may have been headquarters for your family for some time. It can be filled with fond memories, and there can be quite a bit of emotional attachment to it. This can cloud the decision-making ability.

Moving is different, exciting, something to do to perk up retirement. On the other hand, it's a complete break with the past, all the things that have been so close to you for so long. Maybe things aren't so bad rattling around the old homestead after all. And the kids need a place to call home, don't they? And who wants to put up with the headaches of moving?

Don't move for the sake of "doing something." Making a housing decision is a time for sound judgment, not a madcap adventure. Don't stay where you are because you want to hang onto the past. Don't rationalize laziness by perpetuating an "old homestead" myth when you're better off moving somewhere else.

Good reasons for not moving:

- The house fits in with your long-range plans.
- It's convenient to the people and activities that will be the focus of your future.
- You're very happy living where you are.
- The house isn't a financial burden to maintain.
- It would be financially disadvantageous or economically un-feasible to move.
- You want to move to add some excitement to your life.

Good reasons for moving:

- You're hanging in until the real estate market peaks.
- "Proximity to work" is a major attraction of your home.
- Increase in value has been substantial, and you want to realize a profit.
- Housing doesn't meet current or anticipated needs.
- Necessary improvements are too bothersome/costly for you.
- You want to relocate to another area.

- The conditions that attracted you to your property or neighborhood have changed, or your attitudes toward them have.
- You never liked where you're living to begin with.

If you decide pulling up stakes is for you, remain aware of alternative possibilities for altering your housing situation:

- Selling your house
- Renting out your house
- Moving nearby
- Relocating to another part of the country
- Renting real estate
- Buying real estate

If you're going to look for new housing, be professional about it. Conduct research, finding out as much as possible about the general real estate market where you're looking, and about specific individual pieces of property. The following questions will help identify important considerations:

1. Where are we going to look for property?
2. What do we expect out of our property?
3. What are the housing requirements and necessary amenities?
4. How much are we willing to spend?
5. How much are we willing to invest in improvements?
6. How much of our time and energy are we willing to invest in improvements?
7. What is the current status of the real estate market in the area where we want to live?
8. Are property values in the area declining, increasing or stable? Is the current value trend likely to change?
9. How much are we willing to pay for ongoing general maintenance?
10. What independent experts can help us assess the property we select?

Answering these questions will bring you in contact with real estate brokers, contractors, bankers and property owners, and give you a clear picture of what lies ahead. Pay attention to your lifestyle requirements as much as your housing requirements. Make sure activities that are most important to you are available nearby. Try them out. If you're looking at a condo in a golfing community, get out on the links. If you closely follow your investments, visit the local brokerage office. If you enjoy the social whirl you'd better investigate the party circuit.

Consult the appropriate members of your "board of advisors" about any planned move, and if it's far away, start thinking about recruiting new board members. There will be a host of financial considerations. Tax and legal matters must be fully investigated. But try to keep money from being the primary consideration in making a move. First take into account non-financial factors. If they point to making a move, then zero in on the money matters.

With the above caveat in mind, remember the saying about rules being made to be broken—especially when a considerable amount of money is at stake. One executive's home skyrocketed in value over the 25 years his family lived in it. It was larger than they needed with the kids grown-up, but he and his wife liked it, and could afford maintaining it. They planned on moving south when he retired, but at 59, with three years to go, they got "an offer I couldn't refuse," as he put it, for the property. They sold the house, rented a nearby apartment, and plotted their more permanent move.

RELOCATION

Everybody's moving to the sunbelt. Should you move, too? Under no circumstances let inadequacies in your house be the determining factor in a long-distance move. There's no sense in moving to the sunbelt because your house doesn't have enough closet space. If, after careful consideration, you think you want to relocate, experiment first. Try renting in the area before buying. If it's an area you know from vacations, make sure you're comfortable with it in the off-season, as well.

If you're going to relocate, do it because the area you select fits in with your long-range plans. Zero in on the area you want to live in (again, consistent with long-range plans), then look for the right neighborhood, then the right kind of dwelling. One couple followed friends down to Florida, bought a condo, and planned to occupy themselves the way everyone else did—golfing, boating and socializing. He quickly found he didn't care for more than one golf game every other week, she was prone to seasickness, and the social whirl soon became tedious. They're back up North now. He's gone back to work, and they plan to put a lot more thought into their next move.

CASHING IN ON MATURITY

A growing list of businesses and organizations offer discounts on goods and services to maturing individuals. Discounts become available between the ages of 50 and 65, depending on the particular program. Few executives retiring today need to pinch pennies, but they should take advantage of these discount programs whenever possible. Looking into them is an excellent transitional exercise, and thinking about all the cash you can save will give you one more reason to look positively toward the future. Formal discount programs may be offered through club or organization memberships, or discounts may be offered to anyone who can prove they're of a specific age. Investigate which programs and discounts you are eligible for now—or will be in the future. Ask about discounts and special senior services from the following businesses and organizations:

Airlines
American Association of Retired Persons
Banks
Bus Companies
Cultural Institutions and Organizations
Department Stores
Hotels/Motels
Metropolitan Transportation Systems
Movie Theaters
Restaurants
Retail Shops
Travel Clubs and Tour Operators

ACCEPTANCE EXERCISES

1. With your spouse make a list of five long-range goals. Discuss ways to achieve them.

2. Define the activities to which you plan to devote time in retirement.
3. With your spouse, draw up a list of household responsibilities, and indicate which you'll be expected to help with.
4. Gather general information that will help implement post-career plans.
5. Get together socially with a recently retired executive you know.

Disengagement

In the office, Disengagement signals the start of actively reducing management involvement. The counterpart in the home can be thought of as "Engagement." During this stage, you take a more active hand in integrating yourself into your non-career life. You test out plans, rehearse, implement. Here, active attempts to prepare for retirement won't interfere with career management, so they can begin earlier than the three to five years before retirement recommended for Disengagement in the office.

Objectives:

- Finalize post-career plans.
- Begin implementing post-career plans.
- Monitor implementation efforts.
- Adjust and refine plans as necessary.

THE POSITIVE PRINCIPLE

Few managers enjoy talking about retirement. It makes them feel prematurely aged, impotent, living on borrowed time. That these concepts of retirement are dated and obsolete is besides the point; many executives are just plain reluctant to discuss the subject.

If this kind of attitude sounds familiar, get ready to change your behavior. Talking about your plans in a positive context can be tremendously beneficial. The home is an ideal place to put this principle into practice. Here, you can feel free to talk about retirement without worrying about hidden messages co-workers might read into your comments, or fearing that your interest in the future will be misinterpreted as a disregard for your career. With retirement approaching, make a point of bringing it up in a positive context. Tote up the following benefits of mentioning retirement:

- Uses others as a sounding board for your ideas.
- Generates helpful comments and insights from those who may have experience or knowledge you don't possess.
- Overcomes the tendency to view retirement in a negative light.
- Forces you to be aware of your feelings through the process of explaining them to others.
- Builds momentum for plans by involving others in their inception.
- Stimulates interest from and involvement with others, the loss of which is one of retirement's greatest fears.

You don't have to go into a five-minute monologue each time. A simple mention will suffice. If someone asks if you have weekend plans, you might mention you're going down to Howard's sporting goods store to check out a fly rod; when you retire in 18 months you're planning on more fly-fishing, and you're starting to put your gear together now. If the conversation ends there, fine, but it may go on into the subject of fly-fishing, or even retirement itself. Try to bring up the subject in front of as wide a spectrum of people as possible.

Make a positive mention of your retirement at least three times a week. Negative comments have a place, too, but try to save them for one day a week. Write them down first and analyze each. This will help you keep track of the issues that trouble you most. Now you can chart your progress in dealing with them. Be more selective about whom you discuss these issues with; they should be people in a position to help with answers—like your spouse, financial planners, retired executives or a therapist.

By now you and your spouse, and/or anyone else who'll be sharing your future, should have a clear picture of your collective post-career goals, and have an agenda for reaching them. You should formally organize your Corporeal Corporation, and start getting operations up to speed. Make sure you're familiar with the opportunities in each field of operations. The five areas listed below are frequently a part of post-career plans. Now's the time to get ready to make the most of them.

1. Travel
2. Socializing
3. Education
4. Employment
5. Relaxation

Travel

Start making a list of the places you'd like to visit. Talk to travel agents and government tourist boards, and gather information about different tour operators. Get books about places that interest you. Investigate various discount travel clubs that provide steep discounts for travelers with flexible schedules. Get into practice now. When going on business trips, contact departments of tourism and find out about the history and points of interest of your destination, even if you won't have time for them. Getting the big picture of the place you are headed for is good preparation for pleasure traveling in the future.

Socializing

An executive and his wife looked forward to occupying a prominent social position in their community and throwing elegant parties in their recently renovated home. A couple of years before his retirement, they began hosting dinners and parties. He was usually too busy to help with the arrangements, and left the responsibilities to his wife, who was also employed. Both assumed he'd become more involved after his retirement. When the day finally came, it turned out he was no more inclined to pitch in than he was before, creating tension that flared up in the middle of the first lavish bash of his post-career life. The moral of the story: Simulate post-career conditions as closely as possible when you practice your post-career lifestyle. Don't use the excuse that you're too busy to help with research and other necessary work once you've agreed on future plans.

Education

Identify the skills you want to learn or improve, and start looking into the available avenues of instruction. There are many possibilities, and you should investigate them all:

- University courses
- Community learning networks
- Specialized seminars

- Private group instruction
- Private individual instruction
- Apprenticeship
- Self-teaching
- On-the-job training

Keep in mind what you ultimately want from your educational effort. There's nothing wrong with taking art classes because you've always wanted to draw. But if you're taking up a field of study with the thought of generating income, realistically assess the eventual opportunities. An executive who'd enjoyed woodworking as a teenager decided he'd try woodcrafting and cabinetry. He found an ample selection of courses where he could learn on modern equipment and use fine tools. He enrolled in one, and while he enjoyed the course, he wasn't sure if his interest went deep enough to invest in making a home woodworking shop to develop his hobby. His research during Disengagement led him to several local cabinetmakers, one of whom offered to hire him on an as-needed basis. He took the semi-apprenticeship when he retired. He soon learned enough to design and make original bookshelves and tables, using tools he borrowed from his carpenter mentor. He set a goal of selling four of them. His reward, which he soon collected: a complete home woodworking shop.

Employment
If you want to keep working in some capacity after retirement, now's the time to lay the groundwork.

- Develop a network of business contacts who may be able to help you now, or will need your services in the future.
- Have business cards made for yourself.
- Develop a mailing list of potential customers.
- Contact headhunters.
- Mail letters announcing your abilities and availability.
- Investigate teaching opportunities.
- Attend courses or seminars that may strengthen your skills and help make contacts.

Clearly define your reasons for desiring continued employment, and list the various kinds of work available. Other people are out there competing for the same positions you are. Try to differentiate yourself, and know what the competition is doing.

THE RETIREMENT TRANSITION AT HOME   143

An accountant was sure he'd have no trouble making money by handling tax returns and some simple bookkeeping after retirement. His research revealed there were already lots of accountants offering freelance services. He got a personal computer and top-of-the-line software, and began spreading the word about his computerized accounting services, with financial projections included free. Whether it was because of this or not, business picked up quickly.

Relaxation

It's hard downshifting from the hectic pace of a career to a laid-back and unhurried one without getting whiplash. If you define retirement as a time to take it easy, don't confuse this with "doing nothing"—there is no such thing in a successful retirement.

Identify the activities and areas of your current life that will be expanded. Develop alternative plans for new activities in case your anticipated post-career life isn't providing you with enough challenge. Part-time employment or formal instruction are good general alternatives; select the work or learning experience that's right for you. Be ready to go with this plan if you find yourself getting bored, depressed and/or lazy.

POST-CAREER SCHEDULING

Here's a graphic test of your preparation. Project yourself a year into retirement, when you've settled into your planned post-career lifestyle. Imagine yourself during a representative month at your primary residence. Take a monthly planning calendar for the month you've imagined (any year will do). Fill it in. Have a loose schedule for every day of the month. It doesn't have to be an hour by hour format, but identify what you'll be doing in the morning, afternoon and evening. Give yourself the benefit of the doubt. Include activities you've only half-seriously considered, but still aren't sure about pursuing.

You probably won't be able to fill in the month in one sitting, but should work at blocking in a general agenda for each day. How does the month look? Are there any big gaps you can't figure out what to do with? Do you really think you'll want to play bridge four afternoons a week? Will two afternoons a month be enough to keep up with correspondence and paperwork? How many of these activities involve other people, how many involve only yourself? Go over the schedule with your spouse. Get his or her input on whether it seems realistic. Make sure it works for both of you.

If the schedule doesn't look right, identify the problem. Is something missing? What alternative activities can you develop to take up the slack? If you're stuck, look back at your life goals chart. Have you drawn up the best agenda for achieving them? Fine-tune the monthly calendar, adding new activities as you think of them, cutting back on those that won't occupy as much time as you first thought.

The goal of this exercise is not to give you a monthly schedule to follow. It is to make you realize there are a lot of hours in a day, and days in a month. If you can't find something to do with them, they're worse than wasted. The by-product is boredom and depression. But if you can fill up the month with a realistic catalog of involving activities and projects, you'll be able to draw on this wealth of interests 12 months a year.

REVIEWING THE PLANS

Business plans are subject to periodic review, and your personal plans should be, too. Between 10 and 15 years before retirement, review plans no less than every two or three years. Between five and 10 years, biannual or annual reviews are recommended. With less than five years to go, check up on your plans every 12 months. As you review your plans, ask and answer the following questions:

1. Are the goals still the same?
2. What developments have occurred since the last review that need to be taken into account?
3. If the goals are the same, have we made progress toward them?
4. If we haven't made progress, what are the problems and how can we overcome them?
5. If the goals need to be modified, why and how?
6. What developments do we anticipate before the next review that we should be prepared to account for?

LETTING PEOPLE KNOW

When the date of retirement is near, send out announcements to friends and relatives. You'll probably get a few retirement greeting cards in your mailbox, but don't hesitate to post some missives yourself. A few simple words, telling how you wanted to share the happy occasion with them will suffice. If you have future plans you want to tell them about, by all means do.

One executive sent announcements to all his neighbors, saying that he hoped to get to know them better now that he wouldn't be so wrapped up in work. The announcements generated several dinner and social invitations, and an expanded network of friends.

THE RETIREMENT PARTY AT HOME

The office retirement party is an institution. At its core, it's a goodbye, so it's only natural that it's infused with an undercurrent of sadness. For a more uplifting gathering, plan on a retirement party at home. Here, the underlying message is "hello" and "welcome." The guest list should reflect your new lifestyle. Potential partygoers:

- Neighbors you want to get better acquainted with
- Occasional business associates you'd like to develop stronger personal ties with
- Individuals from community groups you plan on spending more time with
- Other retired or soon-to-retire executives
- Good friends you hope to grow even closer to

Avoid packing the party with co-workers or colleagues you probably won't be seeing that much of in the future. If you're not retiring in the traditional sense, but moving from one career into another, starting a business of your own, or switching employers, the "retirement" party is good for business. Make a big splash. Invite potential customers, people who can steer business your way, or contacts who may want to hire you. Put a positive face on your future, and you won't be able to help thinking of it positively. Others will follow your lead and respond the same way.

DISENGAGEMENT EXERCISES

1. Formalize your Corporeal Corporation.
2. Apply for membership in at least one organization in which you receive benefits or discounts based on age alone.

3.   Conduct thorough research on your post-career plans.
4.   Work up a post-career budget.
5.   Make it a point not to bring work home one weekend when you otherwise would.

Ready for the Future

If you're prepared to follow the guidelines laid out for your retirement transition, you'll be in a position to take maximum advantage of the opportunities open to you. But the work isn't finished. Retirement is a beginning, not an end, and it's up to you to keep it moving in the direction you want to go. If you have objectives, and plans for achieving them, you're halfway to your goals. Keep up the good work!

PART IV

MANAGING YOUR HEALTH

Entering pretirement, you've got anywhere from a good 40 to a bad five or less years to enjoy your future, depending on age and health. You can't do anything about your age, but you *can*, to a great degree, control health.

Health management is the first and most basic of your post-career responsibilities. Keeping the physical plant in good condition, and the office upstairs working smoothly, is a top priority for every Corporeal Corporation. Physical health and mental health are linked, and it's your job to keep both systems in shape, working together. If you've never found the time before, get ready to start!

Is Retirement Fatal?

Everybody knows a story about old Joe who keeled over within weeks of retirement. Can retirement really kill you?

We'll answer with a qualified no. There's disagreement about how to interpret statistics and surveys probing the health consequences of retirement. Some argue that, in many cases, it isn't retirement that causes health problems, but health problems that cause retirement. Longitudinal studies are ambiguous about the link, and self-assessment health surveys among retirees tend to elicit overly favorable evaluations, further clouding the issue. Yet even medical experts who hesitate to rush to judgment concede that, statistically, there is an increased risk of death from coronary diseases among recent retirees, especially within the first year of retirement. It is precisely these diseases that are most preventable. While the jury is still out on any direct retirement-health link, it's clear that retirement can be extremely stressful. Those in poor health to begin with, or who aren't prepared to cope with the changes, face a heightened risk of health crises and even death.

If we look beyond the question of retirement and health, and examine overall causes of death, the need for a program of post-career health management becomes even more apparent. In 1900, heart disease and stroke accounted for less than 15% of all fatalities. Today, they are responsible for almost 60%. Many of these deaths can be avoided, and an active and vital life prolonged, with a simple program of health management.

Wellness

People often disregard health until it's threatened by disease. "If it ain't broke, don't fix it" seems to be the attitude about taking steps to preserve well-being. Fortunately, we're seeing this attitude replaced by the concept of "wellness." Instead of waiting for illness to strike, and then getting medical help, wellness emphasizes taking steps to promote continued health. Health management is an ongoing personal wellness program. It has three components:

1. Attitude
2. Fitness
3. Nutrition

If you're skeptical about the benefits of starting your own wellness program, look at what's happening in the workplace. Companies are realizing the bottom-line value of keeping employees in good health. The fitness programs available to executives in only a few select companies a little over a decade ago have spread to all levels of employees in organizations all across the country. Fitness, exercise and other wellness programs save money. The savings per employee resulting from lower insurance payments and increased productivity is estimated to be in the hundreds of dollars. The employee participants also get a bonus; they're more alert, effective, healthy and happy.

As CEO of your Corporeal Corporation, you're also likely to save money by instituting a personal wellness program. Minor expenses of headache pills, antacids and blood pressure medication will add up. Think of the cost of hospitalization if you really let your health management responsibilities slide. But there's more than dollars and cents at stake. Even if insurance paid 100% of your medical bills, the loss of productivity and mental trauma of disease can be devastating, and money alone can never compensate for it. Nor can money match the priceless feeling of control and possibility achieved by conscious efforts to maintain wellness.

Use retirement management skills to design and implement the right personal program for ensuring wellness. Your health management goals during the retirement transition and beyond are as follows:

- Determine current health status.
- Arrest and reverse physical neglect.
- Develop a positive attitude about the future.
- Control physical and psychological stresses of transition.
- Gather information about health and health management: benefit and medical plans, checkups, insurance.
- Make plans for future health maintenance.

The Health Partnership

Your relationship with your physician or other primary health care provider will become increasingly important in the years ahead. Developing a health partnership with your doctor fosters a feeling of control that will help you stay involved with managing your health. A bond of trust and communication is essential, and one that's too often ignored. The average person spends more than twice as much time in finding the least expensive supermarket than in selecting a doctor. Which do you think is a more important choice? If you haven't developed this kind of relationship, make efforts to create one, either with your present physician or another.

The health partnership isn't a 50-50 deal. You are the senior partner. Your doctor is your subordinate. He's an accountant for your health. Your body bears the record of how operations have been running, and he checks the records and makes recommendations. You should plan to make maximum use of his expertise, but ultimately, maintaining health is your responsibility. We tend to put doctors on pedestals—to our own detriment. It makes us think that only a specialist has the power to do anything about our health. We have our bodies examined as though we are passive observers. Involve yourself not only in maintaining health, but also in medical evaluations and decisions.

Checkups

Some medical authorities have charged that annual physical examinations are a waste of time and money. Yet the annual physical checkup is an excellent method of keeping tabs on your health and helping you focus on wellness throughout the year. This annual rite becomes increasingly important as retirement age approaches. Components of a thorough annual physical examination include chest X-ray, blood profile, complete blood count, blood pressure reading, electrocardiogram, urinalysis, and test for occult blood in the stool. A colonoscopy may be done every two years.

To get the most out of your periodic exams, prepare for them mentally. Spend at least one hour over the preceding month developing a list of questions about your health, nutrition, exercise and other medical issues (don't let this keep you from seeking answers from other legitimate sources, as well). The other talents of your physician notwithstanding, he isn't a mind reader. You may have questions about changes in sleeping patterns or diet. Perhaps you've been feeling more stressed lately, and wonder about the consequences. Ask for health maintenance recommendations based on your medical history.

A doctor's time is in heavy demand. When you call to schedule or confirm your appointment, make it clear you'll want to talk to the doctor, not just be examined, and make sure sufficient time is allotted to discuss your questions.

CHAPTER TEN

ATTITUDE

Attitude has a direct bearing on physical health. The connection has moved from the realm of folklore to scientific fact, as researchers have zeroed in on the link between the brain and the immune system. The American Psychological Association recently came out in support of the notion, and there are literally thousands of studies in medical literature backing up the relationship between mental attitude and disease.

While most studies in this area have focused on how attitude affects recovery from a specific disease, research also indicates proper mental attitude can prevent illness from occurring. A study at Ohio State university found the stress surrounding academic examinations led to measurable declines in students' immune systems, leaving them more susceptible to colds and flu. Which do you think is more stressful: final exams or retirement?

Attitude is not immutable. If you suffer from negative thinking, or a dour outlook, you can learn to improve your attitude. Clinical studies have proven patients suffering from an array of stress-related disorders—including coronary conditions, hypertension, chronic headaches, and gastrointestinal disorders—can be taught progressive relaxation techniques, yoga and stress-reduction exercises. There are a wealth of books, classes and other instruction available to teach you these techniques. Make finding this information, and putting it to work for you, one of your health management projects.

Keeping a positive attitude about yourself and the future can help you achieve any dynamic scenario you envision. The difference between positive and negative attitudes is the same as the difference between success and failure. Think positive. Retirement is an opportunity to have more control over your life than you've every had before.

Retirement

Positive Attitudes	Negative Attitudes
Prepare you for success.	Can precipitate a health crisis.
Motivate you.	Distort your view of future
Keep you optimistic.	possibilities.
Allow you to unleash your full	Prevent you from fully exploring
potential.	your options.
Give you the strength to make	Keep you from devoting full
necessary changes.	energy to your future agenda.
Help you maintain health.	Lick you before you get started.
Get results.	Become self-fulfilling
Make life worth living.	prophecies.

Attitude and Stress

Stress has won a starring role as a villain in the wellness picture, but in fact it has been miscast. Everyone needs some stress in their lives, but the optimum level is different for each person. Stress is the body's response to change, and it can be beneficial or harmful, depending on its source and your ability to deal with it.

Retirement, whether or not you're looking forward to it, is a major change in life, and therefore creates a great deal of stress. So do many other positive situations, like getting a promotion, giving a speech, even going on vacation. Exercise also causes stress. On the downside, having a deal go sour, being annoyed with co-workers, or a family crisis, can create negative stress. Controlling stress means cultivating healthy sources of stress, while working to reduce unhealthy sources, and learning to cope with negative stress that can't be avoided.

Attitude and stress share a close association. Attitude filters our perceptions. A poor attitude can transform a minor inconvenience into a major source of stress, while a positive and healthy attitude can help us deal with a highly negative stress.

There are two sources of stress: physical and psychological.

Physical Stress

The stress we get from moderate physical exertion is healthy. If your system isn't subjected to this kind of stress, it begins to weaken and atrophy. Exercise elevates the blood pressure, keeps muscles limber and strengthens the heart. If you exercise regularly, your body is better able to handle sources of unhealthy stress, either disease or negative psychological stress.

Psychological Stress

Psychological stress provokes many of the same physiological responses as physical stress: blood pressure rises, the heart starts beating faster, adrenaline is secreted, we may begin to sweat. But some things happen with psychological stress that don't happen with physical stress. Among them is the release of the hormone cortisol, which blocks the removal of acids in the bloodstream. Over time, the elevated acid levels can wreak havoc on the stomach lining. Voila, an ulcer. Eventually, uncontrolled psychological stress can also exacerbate circulatory and cardiac problems, and cause death. That's one reason why it's better to have your heart thumping when you're doing laps in a swimming pool that while you're sitting in your office worrying about your future.

STRESS-RELATED DISEASES

Uncontrolled stress can kill. That's why it's imperative to work to control it. Stress contributes to the onset of virtually all mental and physical health problems. It is a major cause of high blood pressure, or hypertension, which in turn leads to coronary disease by increasing the heart's workload—it has to pump hard to keep pressure at elevated levels. High blood pressure has reached epidemic proportions. Research shows hypertension can cause problems at much lower pressure levels than previously believed. The American Heart Association recently lowered its estimate of what constitutes high blood pressure, from 160/95 to 140/90.

High blood pressure is treatable through diet, exercise and medication. Medication is the method of choice for many executives, but when alternatives exist it's the least desirable. Some of the drugs that have been used extensively to control high blood pressure are now suspected of having adverse side effects. A sound wellness program is the best way to stave off stress-related disease of all kinds.

RETIREMENT STRESS

How do you know if you'll face retirement-related stress? How you handle stress today provides a partial answer. So does your degree of confidence about the future, your expectations and how realistic they are. The more you prepare and know what to expect, the less stress you'll face in retirement. Recognizing problem areas beforehand will help you design adaptation strategies for dealing with them. Developing a complete business plan for the future will minimize the uncertainty ahead. As one CEO put it, "The thing that gets me the most stressed is uncertainty . . . I'm a firm believer that worrying about the uncertainty is worse than learning the facts."

Since uncertainty creates unhealthy stress, and unhealthy stress has adverse consequences, make efforts to minimize retirement uncertainty. Uncertainty begins to manifest itself within the decade preceding retirement, and increases in intensity as the actual date approaches.

If you're between 10 and five years away from retirement, be able to make the following statements with assurance:

1. I have solid ideas about my post-career plans.
2. I plan on seeking more information and help with my retirement decisions.
3. I'm beginning to view retirement as a time for new opportunities and growth.

4. I'm aware of my ability to deal with stress in my career, and plan on using this ability in retirement.

If retirement is between five years and 18 months away, be able to make the following statements with assurance:

1. I've been paying attention to my health to ensure a lifetime of vitality.
2. I've discussed retirement benefits and other "hard" issues with the personnel office or other appropriate officials.
3. I've gathered information on post-career budget and finances.
4. I'm organizing my retirement advisory board.
5. I've involved those close to me in post-career decisions.
6. I'm beginning to look beyond my career, and honestly feel there are many new challenges ahead.
7. I've learned to be aware of and control the sources of stress in my life.

If you are within 18 months of retirement, be able to make the following statements with assurance:

1. My post-career plans have been solidified, and I have alternative plans prepared for contingency situations.
2. I am completing projects and other career business so I will be able to face the future without looking back.
3. I have started rehearsing or simulating important aspects of my post-career life.
4. My retirement advisory board is organized.
5. I have realistically evaluated the potential problem areas in my plans.
6. My post-career housing situation has been evaluated.
7. I have reduced my management responsibilities and/or emotional commitment to my career.

STRESS IN THE HOME

Even managers who've learned to handle stress in the executive suite can encounter significant problems in coping with the stress of retirement. How much effort do you put into controlling stress in the home, and what are its principle causes? Getting some answers can put you on the road to reducing non-career stress today, and post-career stress tomorrow.

NON-CAREER STRESS EVALUATION

1. In the last month, what are the five things that caused you the most aggravation at home? Were they resolved? How?
2. Are there ongoing points of contention between you and your spouse? What are they, and how is retirement likely to affect them?
3. If you and your spouse have an argument, what is the typical way it will be resolved?
4. When something bothers you, how do you deal with it?
5. How effective are you at handling the minor irritations of everyday life?
6. If you find yourself feeling tense or anxious, how adept are you at determining the cause of your feelings?
7. How easy is it for you to admit you're wrong, and apologize, if the situation warrants it?

Attitude, Stress and Management Personality

This is a good time to review the evaluation of your management personality, since the four problem personalities described earlier exhibit attitudes that can create high levels of negative stress in retirement, and adversely impact on attitude. If you exhibit characteristics of these personality types, plan on closely monitoring your attitude and sources of stress, and prepare to implement strategies to deal with associated adjustment problems.

Reactive Manager
Provide an alternate to stimulation currently found in career; second career, continued employment, very involved hobby are good outlets. If starting your own business, keep Reactive tendencies in check to minimize interference with success. Avoid temptation to become heavily involved with "management" of your home if you haven't been involved before; chances are your input will create more problems than it solves, unless your involvement is thoroughly discussed and agreed upon beforehand.

Overachiever

Seek activities providing external competition currently provided by career; organized sports, fundraising, part-time sales positions are good sources of positive competition. Build goals into personal projects, e.g., exercise programs, projects around the house. Without being compulsive, keep informed of what retired colleagues are up to, and "compete" with them by trying to make your post-career years even more satisfying and fulfilling than theirs.

Company Man

Develop sources of external direction. Discuss plans and objectives with family and friends to create group decision-making structure. Seek help from your board of advisors. Join organized activities that will make you feel part of a team. If necessary, investigate maintaining periodic contact with former colleagues and/ or company to minimize subconscious feelings of abandonment. Maintain a list of long-range projects, and periodically review your performance in realizing them.

Combat Vet

Work through the stress associated with post-combat syndrome. Part-time employment can make you feel capable and in command again. Seek experiences that will put you in touch with your feelings; acting with community theater groups, classes in painting and sculpture, or poetry are helpful. Volunteer work can be beneficial, especially if it involves children, the disabled or disadvantaged, or other populations that will look up to you and make you appreciate how much you really have. Work at developing a schedule of meaningful activities to keep you involved and active.

CHAPTER ELEVEN

FITNESS

"People who are active and fit can expect to live a year or so longer than their sedentary counterparts. For each hour of physical activity, you can expect to live that hour over—and live one or two more hours to boot."
—Dr. Ralph Paffenbarger, Jr.,
Stanford University School of Medicine

It's official. After years of study and dispute, studies now prove that exercise can increase longevity. But there's a lot more to fitness than tacking a year or more onto your life. Being fit dramatically improves the quality of life. We feel more capable, more alert, more in control of ourselves, more *alive* when we're fit.

For the executive approaching retirement, fitness is especially important. First, at around the age of 50, the physiological changes associated with aging begin to manifest themselves. A fitness program can stave off and even reverse these changes. Secondly,

161

regular exercise helps maintain a positive attitude for dealing with pretirement stress.

How fit do you have to be to stay healthy? How much exercise do you need? These are two different questions. To answer the first one, aerobic exercise three times a week is considered sufficient to promote cardiovascular health. Aerobic means "achieve in the presence of oxygen," but forget the technicalese; an aerobic activity is one that raises your energy output and requires your heart to pump faster and breathing to be deeper and/or faster for a minimum of 20 minutes. How do you know if an activity is increasing your respiratory rate to aerobic levels? A general formula for a target heartbeat rate is 70% of 220 minus age. Swimming, jogging and jumping rope are examples of aerobic exercises. Tennis and basketball aren't, because the activity isn't constant. Devote one pure hour a week to fitness (3 X 20 minutes), and you can achieve cardiovascular health.

The amount of exercise you need may be different from the amount of exercise necessary to promote cardiovascular health. Physical activity and exercise can be rewarding in themselves, but you may need more involvement and positive feelings than you get from a bare-bones aerobic program. You may need to develop a more comprehensive regimen to compensate for competitive urges formerly satisfied in your career. Or you may need to socialize in group exercise programs if you miss the camaraderie of your job. Defining what you want, as well as what you need, out of a fitness program is the first step to designing a successful regimen.

Of course, part of a successful program involves finding an activity you enjoy that is readily available on an ongoing basis. Take care in selecting an exercise that fits the bill.

Common Aerobic Exercises

Walking	Rowing
Jogging	Cross Country Skiing
Swimming	Bicycling
Aerobic Dancing/Calisthenics	

Fitness and Career

If you don't exercise regularly but your company provides on-site facilities, privileges at a private facility or club, or other wellness or fitness programs, take advantage of them. Initiating a fitness program during Pretirement is an excellent transitional exercise. External encouragement and structure can be a real boost in overcoming inertia, one more reason to get started now, rather than later when you have to go it alone. If you're going to retire soon, and figure you'll wait until then to start exercising, reconsider your delaying tactics. It's much easier to continue a program, no matter how modest, that's already been started, than to start one from scratch. Additionally, an activity that connects your career to retirement gives you a feeling of continuity that makes the transition easier.

Fitness isn't medicine. It's fun and it tastes good. Remember the money you're saving from your wellness program? Divert the cash into your activity development fund. Set aside a few hundred dollars, or a few thousand, to invest in sports equipment, horseback riding, lessons in dance or martial arts. Exercise doesn't have to be aerobic to be fun and invigorating. Sure, you want to keep your heart in top shape, but don't forget your spirits! It feels good to use all your muscles, try new things, and spend that cash you've earned by taking care of yourself.

Those whose companies don't have an exercise or fitness program should develop their own. Keep these guidelines in mind:

Fitness Programs

Should	Should Not
Have tangible goals.	Be compulsive.
Provide tangible rewards.	Be overly demanding.
Have measurable success.	Be painful.
Be enjoyable.	Be inconvenient.
Be realistic.	Be inconsistent.

Some executives are enamored of quick results at the expense of long-range goals during their careers. Despite financial incentives geared to long-term growth, they may concentrate on immediate successes that keep the boss, shareholders or Wall Street money managers happy. This management mindset can sabotage efforts to promote personal fitness. Make sure you use long-range strategic planning when developing your wellness program (and all its components). Decide (with proper input from appropriate members of your board, of course) what your goals are, and make sure you give yourself adequate time to get there.

If you're in poor health now, it's probably the result of poor health management practices developed over many years. Expecting to turn operations around overnight is unrealistic, and sets you up for failure. Look at your program in the long term.

Fitness to Go

Don't let business travel and erratic schedules stop your exercise regimen. Take your fitness program on the road. Many hotels have exercise facilities or pools, or offer privileges at nearby health clubs. Some even provide maps of nearby jogging trails. Make it a point to stay at hotels with such facilities or privileges, even if you don't think you'll have the time, or don't plan to use them. Making the effort to have reservations at healthy hotels will reinforce the idea of the benefits of exercise. Bring exercise gear with you even if you don't think you'll have the time to use it. Maybe one of your meetings will get canceled. And what if, in a fit of conscience, you decide it would be a lot better to take a walk or jog instead of sitting in the bar? Get a map of the city beforehand, and see if there are interesting areas to walk through, or if it's possible to walk to any of your meetings.

Your credit card may be as good as a health club membership. For example, Diners Club and American Express platinum cardholders have entree to health facilities in major cities around the country. More of these on-the-road fitness opportunities are opening up daily. Make it a point to keep abreast of them, again reinforcing fitness as an important concern. If you become knowledgeable about various facilities available to you when you travel, you're more likely to take advantage of them.

A Post-career Exercise Program

If you're out of shape and in retirement, or about to retire, and plan on exercising without benefit of an organized program, be especially careful in planning your regimen. Retired executives, without a career to prove themselves in, and with the subliminal message of being "over the hill," often use the field of physical fitness for showing the world they've still got it. Taken to the extreme, this is dangerous. Crash fitness programs usually do exactly that: They crash, leaving a trail of bruised bodies, deflated spirits and potentially fatal coronary complications. Don't let your fitness fantasy get out of hand. In moderation it can be a powerful motivation, an effective way of exerting control over one's environment and overcoming fears of aging and inadequacy. Once a modest program is ignited, the feelings of health and vitality are enough to sustain and build the flames of enthusiasm.

SCHEDULING

Executives often use their schedules as an excuse for not exercising. It's true that the dictates of a career can make it more difficult to find time for fitness. But in retirement *you* make the schedule, and this plays an important part in the overall success of your fitness program. The time of day can greatly affect your body's response, and how pleasurable the exercise is. Some people are at a physical peak in the morning. Others are at their friskiest in the afternoon or evening, or prefer keeping a schedule flexible so they can work around other post-career commitments. Experiment with exercising at various time to learn the hours you find most convenient and enjoyable.

One of the greatest advances in executive health in recent years has been the jogging suit. Its acceptance means you can look great while you're exercising to feel great. Moreover, it's versatile—wear it for exercise or for running errands around town. This can play a part in finding your optimum exercise hour. Set aside three days during the next week when you'll have no pressing business. On these days, put on a clean jogging suit as your clothes for the day. Make a commitment to engage in your chosen exercise activity at some point during the day, be it on an exercise bike or taking a vigorous walk, but don't decide what time that will be beforehand. All you have to do is make sure you do this sometime before you go to sleep. You'll probably find a time in the day you're naturally drawn to; perhaps midmorning, maybe in the cool of the evening. Or you can just experiment with exercising at different times. See which you like the most. If you exercise at a health club, you might want to choose the time when exercise equipment is least crowded. Or, if you're gregarious, you may opt for a time when more people are around, and engage in a bit of socializing while you're improving your health. For some, involvement with others may be a prerequisite for a successful program. If you have trouble motivating yourself, develop a buddy system for exercising with someone. This outside impetus can help you get started and keep going. The same goes for scheduled exercise classes. If you need outside help, make sure you get it.

Consider scheduling your exercise to preempt a less healthy activity. If you're overimbibing during cocktail hour, try exercising instead.

FITNESS NOTES

You're only a few pounds overweight, and you don't plan on doing anything too strenuous to start with. You don't really need to get a thorough physical exam before starting a fitness program, right? Wrong!

Even those who seem to be in excellent health may have serious cardiac problems that can only be detected with a complete examination. Besides, executives tend to overrate their fitness. One study of over 2,000 mid- to top-level executives found that over 90% claimed they were in good to excellent health, yet less than half of them reported they exercised regularly. That means almost half of them contradicted themselves. Additionally, no matter what shape you're in, a complete exam will establish the baseline from which you'll measure your improvement.

Physiological changes associated with aging must also be taken into account when exercising. The body's thermostat has less ability to regulate internal temperature, and there's a decreased ability to perspire. Medication can further impair body temperature regulation. To compensate, avoid exercise in hot, muggy weather, and wear light clothing when it's warm. Conversely, in cold weather, wear clothing that will help retain body heat.

The most dangerous period may be right after you exercise. If you stop suddenly, without cooling down, your blood pressure and pulse rate quickly drop, but hormones that stimulate cardiac activity are still high. The overstimulated heart, without an adequate supply of blood, can develop fatal abnormalities in rhythm. Gradually slow down or reduce your intensity, instead of finishing with a big kick or burst of energy and collapsing while you catch your breath.

Exercise: The General Rules

1. Don't exercise when you don't feel well.
2. If you've stopped for over a week, gradually build back up to your previous level of performance.
3. You should feel better, not worse, after you exercise.
4. Avoid exercise in extreme weather.
5. Drink plenty of fluids in warm weather—water is best.
6. "No pain, no gain," makes no sense.

The warning signs of overexercise are:

- Unfamiliar discomfort in the neck, chest, arm, jaw, shoulder or upper abdomen during or right after exercise.
- Weakness or shortness of breath.
- Tightness in the chest or throat

The Myth of Mental Decline

Fears of mental decline often haunt the maturing executive. He forgets someone's name, the details of a deal slip his mind. Suddenly he wonders if he's losing his memory, getting senile. Yet the maturing executive has as much mental capacity, and in some cases even more, than he did when he was younger. Momentary lapses of memory occur at all ages. Yet concern about this common occurrence create anxiety that will have a detrimental effect on mental performance. Among those physically and emotionally healthy, the exercise of mental powers can continue virtually un-diminished into the 80s.

Loss of memory or mental abilities isn't a normal part of aging. When it does happen, it is most often caused by the side effects of medication. Consult your physician if you suspect mental impairment, and attempt to trace its cause. In most cases, a decline in mental abilities is reversible.

THE TWO KINDS OF INTELLIGENCE

Mental capacity is defined by two kinds of intelligence:

1. Crystallized Intelligence
2. Fluid Intelligence

Crystallized intelligence is the ability to use a reservoir of knowledge to make decisions and render judgment. It's "experience" in simple terms, and our ability to learn from it. Crystallized intelligence is used for solving a problem with a range of options, rather than a clear-cut answer. Increments in the growth of crystallized intelligence get smaller as we age, but crystallized intelligence nonetheless continues to grow. Verbal intelligence can also increase throughout life.

Fluid intelligence is the ability to manipulate abstract patterns and relationships. Playing chess is an example. There is a minor (some medical experts say "inconsequential") decline in fluid intelligence with age, but this may be more than compensated for by experience. Some experts further assert that the cognitive tests which measure fluid intelligence are biased in favor of the young, and that fluid intelligence doesn't decline at all.

Scientists on the cutting edge of brain research say brain cell growth continues late in life. Yet improvements in mental ability, or even its maintenance, aren't automatic. Like every other part of the body, the brain needs exercise and stimulation to remain healthy. Make it a point to remain mentally active, seek new experiences and avoid routine whenever possible. This becomes even more important during post-career years when you don't have the new mental challenges your career constantly provided.

> "Nerve cells can grow at any age in response to intellectual enrichment of all sorts: travel, crossword puzzles, anything that stimulates the brain with novelty and challenge."
> —Dr. Marian Diamond, University of California at Berkeley

MENTAL EXERCISES

1. Take a different route when you drive home or to a frequent destination.

2. Shop or browse in a store you've never been in.
3. Try a new restaurant.
4. Buy and look through three magazines you've never read before.
5. Watch a TV program you've never seen.
6. Take a course that requires reading and/or class discussion.

CHAPTER TWELVE

NUTRITION

What would you think of a company that wasted time and money turning out a product that you knew could be produced better, cheaper and faster? You'd probably give low marks to the management of the operation, and wonder how they stay in business. Yet this is the kind of management many executives exercise in providing for their own nourishment. They favor fried foods and rich gravies and sauces that require not only time, but also multiple pots and pans for preparation. Good, nutritious and appetizing food is generally cheaper, easier to prepare, and quicker to clean up after, than elaborate and unhealthy meals.

Before we proceed, let us state unequivocally that there's more to food than its nutritional value—eating is one of life's most pleasurable activities. The goal is not to consume the necessary nutrients in the least amount of time possible in order to spend time on more "productive" tasks. However, there's little sense in devoting time and attention to orchestrating a diet that you know is fundamentally detrimental to your health.

More companies are realizing the importance of nutrition as part of wellness, and are going all out to make the food in snack machines, company cafeterias and executive dining rooms more healthy. Sure, there are a few comments about "rabbit food" at first, as the president of a small Midwestern lumber company observed after upgrading the on-site nutritional standards, but people soon realize good eating habits aren't draconian. Some of the largest companies in the country are hiring food consultants to create healthy and appetizing menus. They're also sponsoring seminars on nutrition, so people can take their new appreciation for good eating home with them.

> "We have to get people away from the idea that if they change their nutritional habits they have to spend all their time in health food stores. We show them that if 80 percent of their food is decent and nourishing, 20 percent can still be big Macs or ice cream or potato chips."
> —Nancy Love, Corporate Food Consultant, NutriWork

Good Food

What exactly is "good" food? It's part of a diet that both your taste buds and your body enjoy. It isn't necessarily one dish and not another, but a collection of meals and snacks that are low in fat, sugar and sodium, sufficiently fibrous, and provide the necessary vitamins, minerals and calories, while keeping you at a healthy weight. This is not a description of the typical American diet. The average diet is filled with too much fat and sugar and not enough complex carbohydrates. A standard nutritional recommendation in a field rife with dissension is that a healthy diet should be two-thirds from plant sources and one-third from animal sources. The average diet is exactly the opposite.

After that, nutritionally speaking, the subject of good food can get as complicated as you want. Bookstores are packed with books on nutrition, magazines are devoted to it. There are nutritional guidelines for people who won't eat anything but fruits, nuts and grains, and others that promise weight loss and health while dining on whatever you're eating now. There's pretty solid agreement that we know very little about food and nutrition, and that each individual's body has its own unique requirements for and reactions to various foods—good or otherwise.

Learning about what you're eating, and what you should be eating, is a fundamental part of health management. Make it a major project. Consult professional dietitians and nutritionists, and investigate a range of literature. Remember that "good" food is enjoyable, and includes an occasional excess. Food that's enjoyable to eat should also be enjoyable to prepare, and readily available. It should provide a wide range of dishes to avoid monotony and provide the greatest range of nutrients. (Another point of agreement in the nutritional community is that we probably don't know all the vitamins we get from food, so the wider the variety, the more vitamins.)

Nutrition is especially important during the retirement transition and retirement, because the body's nutrient requirements begin changing at around age 50. Eating habits have to be modified accordingly.

The Basic Rules of Nutritional Management

1. Evaluate your eating habits and patterns.
2. Define your nutritional attitudes and practices.
3. Assess eating habits and patterns of others in your household.
4. Identify the benefits of an improved nutritional program.
5. Identify the drawbacks of continued poor nutrition.
6. Involve others in a sound nutrition program.
7. Modify eating behavior, not just the food you eat.
8. Design a healthy, well-planned nutritional program that takes your palate and lifestyle into account.
9. Avoid compulsive dietary regimens.
10. Set goals and rewards for improving dietary habits.

Eating Habits

To control nutrition you have to know your current eating habits; this goes beyond vitamins, minerals and meals. As stated earlier, eating is more than nutrition. We eat for celebration, we eat because we're with friends, when we're bored, or when we want to avoid doing something else. We can develop bad habits, using food in self-destructive, though instantly gratifying ways. What are you using food for?

EVALUATING EATING HABITS

The following exercises will help you identify your eating habits more clearly. Get out a paper and pen, and put your answers to the following questions in writing:

1. How have your eating habits and attitudes about food changed during your adult years? Describe your eating habits over the past year. How much attention do you give to your nutrition and eating habits today?
2. Write down everything you remember eating, chronologically, in the last seven days. Was this an unusual week of eating? If so, what made it unusual?
3. How far in advance do you plan when and what you'll eat? How do your eating patterns at home differ from those while at work or traveling?

Keep a log of everything you eat during a seven-day period. Note the time you ate it, why you ate it, and what you were doing while you ate it. Evaluate how much you enjoyed the experience, and what it was about the experience you enjoyed. For example, if you were with people, was it the company and conversation you enjoyed, or was it that superb Madeira sauce on the capon? If you were grabbing a bite in your office or at your desk, were you reading or just enjoying the food? Make entries in a small notebook and record your thoughts as soon after each eating event as possible.

Divide a sheet of paper in half. Label the top of one half "Attitudes," the other "Practices." Write 10 statements about food that describe your attitudes and practices under each. For example:

Attitudes	*Practices*
Convenience is more important than nutrition.	I stick to my favorite foods.
Real men don't eat health food.	I stop eating before I'm full.
The way food looks is as important as how it tastes.	I dislike trying new things.
Nutritious food is boring.	I have a cocktail to unwind almost every evening.
We should eat to live, not live to eat.	I always seem to be on a diet.
	We keep plenty of healthy snack foods on hand.

Attitudes	Practices
We are what we eat. I'm not convinced diet and health are related.	If everyone else is having dessert I can't pass it up. When there's nothing else to do, I eat.

Looking over your answers will help you identify the specifics of your eating pattern. If you need to change your nutritional habits, this is the first step to getting food under control. Improper eating habits are a behavioral problem as well as a nutritional one. Modify eating behavior, not just the food you eat. Examine the log of your current eating habits, the when and why of your eating events, to identify situations that trigger eating. You may be a:

Schedule eater—Always have meals and snacks at the same time.
Stress eater—Grab something to munch on or overeat when you're under the gun or upset.
Ritual eater—Have coffee or snack when you go into a meeting or sit down for a series of calls, or always plan social events around food.

Identifying the when and why of any problem behavior helps correct it. Knowing what triggers your eating is a big step toward controlling it. We translate a variety of feelings into hunger for psychological reasons. Hunger is an easier feeling to satisfy than more unsettling issues that we often interpret as hunger.

Food Control

The pressures of pretirement exacerbate bad eating habits. Food and alcohol are a quick source of solace. These behaviors and habits can quickly get out of hand during retirement. There's more time to eat, drink and be merry, and less incentive to curb our appetites. Retirement's supposed to be enjoyable, right? Why not freshen up that cocktail, or have another slice of pie? A few months of this kind of behavior, and you'll know why.

You need the support and involvement of the entire household to give a program of nutritional change the best chance of success. It's hard to avoid temptation when there are cheeze woozles, hickory stix, and heaven knows what else being munched and crunched all around you. Involve the family in a discussion about nutrition, and habits that need to be changed.

Identify the benefits of an improved nutritional program prior to meeting with family members. Be ready to present your thoughts with everyone gathered, and solicit positive comments that will help generate an atmosphere of constructive change. Typical benefits:

- Improved health
- New appreciation of food
- Financial savings
- More group responsibility and participation in menu planning

Identify the drawbacks of continued poor nutrition. Discuss the downside of continued poor nutritional habits. Children still living at home are often unimpressed by sound nutrition. They may resent having to give up their favorite "junk food" because mom or dad has gone on a health kick. Perhaps they want to be able to offer friends cheeze woozles instead of a carrot stick when they come over. Even if they or your spouse don't share your newfound zeal, explaining the problems of poor nutrition usually elicits encouragement of your efforts to shape up, and that can be a big boost in the battle of the bulge. Typical drawbacks of poor nutrition:

- Contributes to health problems.
- Puts a strain on the system.
- Costs more.
- Makes one feel tired and bloated.

A simple method of controlling eating: Never eat alone while doing anything else; don't read, don't watch TV, don't listen to the radio. Too often, eating while doing something else expands to fill the available time. The right kind of food doesn't need any accompaniment. It should provide enough interest in its taste, and to your hand in creating it, to stand on its own.

Keep goals and rewards within your overall health incentive program. It can take the form of a cash incentive contributed to your activity development fund. Weight loss is a tangible measurement of success for an overweight individual. But hopping on the scale every day can be depressing if you take the correct (slow and steady) approach to weight control. Other goals that can be measured include the number of days you eat only nutritionally sound meals. Goals can be based on a combination of total calories consumed and calories expended in your fitness program. Provide intermediate rewards. If you want to drop five pounds in six weeks, give yourself weekly bonuses for sticking to the regimen, and the grand prize when you reach the goal. Repeat as necessary.

NUTRITIONAL MANAGEMENT EXERCISES

- Go to a bookstore and look through books devoted to healthy eating. There will be a large selection, and you should have no trouble finding one that addresses nutrition from the level of involvement you're willing to devote to it. Buy it and read it.
- Buy an appliance that will help with the preparation of healthy meals. A juicer that makes juice from vegetables as well as from fruits is ideal. A wok is also an ideal cooking implement to invest in.
- Plan an imaginary seven-day menu that provides all your favorite foods. Next, plan an imaginary seven-day menu that you think would be ideal from a long-term health perspective. Take these menus, along with your one-week food log, to a nutritionist. Together, design a realistic, appetizing and healthy one-week menu.
- Shop and prepare, or assist in the shopping and preparation of, the one-week menu you planned.

ROAD FOOD

Some executives use constant, or even occasional travel as an excuse for deficiencies in the nutritional department (just as they excuse their avoiding exercise). You gulp down coffee to get going and stay awake, grab a bite when you get a chance, dine on airplane food, and aren't sure when or what you'll be eating next. Business meals mean business, entertaining too often means excess.

The demise of the three-martini lunch was a good start, but most executives have yet to master nutritional management. The good news is, it's easier than ever and more socially acceptable for executives to practice sound nutritional management. More restaurants and hotel chains catering to the business crowd offer low-calorie, low-fat items and meals on the menu. Cathedrals of power dining offer executives a selection of items identified as "Spa Cusine," or designate special sections of the menu for health-minded fare.

Major hotel chains catering to business travelers are changing their dining room and coffee shop menus to reflect new interest in nutrition. If this food isn't available where you're staying, or you plan on eating elsewhere, ask at the desk about nearby restaurants with salad bars or low-fat menus. When ordering food, get into the habit of asking how dishes are prepared. Waiters are attuned to the development of lighter palates, and the kitchen can often alter recipes or lighten up on sauces if you request it.

You don't have to worry that people will perceive you as a health fanatic for asking these questions; if anything, you'll be regarded as ahead of the pack. Asking about food preparation or the location of restaurants with low-calorie menus will help you keep focused on the benefits of nutrition, and make it that much easier for you to develop good eating habits. on the road and at home.

AVOID FANATICISM

Few people are more boring than zealots. If you've suddenly seen the light, have patience with those less enlightened. Don't make disparaging comments about fatty or sugared foods others are eating. Don't cringe if someone suggests going out for a steak. Leave your calorie counter book at home on occasion. Don't insist that red meat not be kept in the same refrigerator with your bean sprouts.

Nutrition and Retirement

The importance of nutritional management increases with age. The digestive system can't handle fat, sugar, alcohol and caffeine like it used to. The body can't burn off the excess calories as easily. And dietary requirements change. Nutrients aren't absorbed as readily, and we need different amounts of vitamins and minerals.

Precisely how much our dietary needs change is unknown, but researchers studying the question made some disturbing related discoveries: Many of those over 65 are suffering from some degree of malnutriton. The estimates run from 15% to 50% of the population and, as one researcher went out of his way to point out, "These numbers hold up even among affluent white populations, especially in cases of specific micronutrients (vitamins and minerals)."

A basic problem is that while the need for nutrients remains relatively close to that of earlier years, the need for calories declines, because we generally expend less energy as we age. A well-balanced diet is more important than ever to get the necessary nutrients without getting the excess calories that aren't easy to burn up. Unless you manage your diet, you may eat lots of calories you don't need to get the nutrients you do; you'll quickly gain weight. Conversely, changes in the sense of taste and smell can lead to reduced appetite. You might not gain weight, but you'll very likely suffer a vitamin or mineral deficiency. This can trigger a lower immune response and other problems previously associated with aging, which are now believed to be more linked to poor nutrition.

Drugs can also wreak havoc with diet by altering appetite, or the ability of the body to absorb nutrients. By some estimates, four out of five people over the age of 60 take drugs for chronic ailments. If you're one of them, find out the side effects of any medication you use.

VITAMINS

If it's hard to get all the nutrients you need from food, why not take vitamins? It might seem a sensible alternative, but there's disagreement about the body's ability to absorb nutrients packaged in pills and capsules. Additionally, since there's growing agreement that all the vitamins and minerals we get from a well-balanced diet haven't been identified, it stands to reason they can't all be found in vitamin pills.

Your doctor may recommend vitamin and mineral supplements because of a special diet or digestive problem. Also, women may need calcium supplements to prevent osteoporosis. It's unwise to put yourself on a vitamin or supplement regimen without consulting a physician. Overmedication is a problem, particularly with the trend toward "megavitamins" that may contain 10 to 100 times daily recommended allowances of some vitamins and minerals. Too much of a good thing can be as bad as not enough. Vitamin A overdoses can cause headaches, diarrhea, nausea, and liver, kidney and bone damage. Too much iron can build up to harmful levels in the liver. Vitamin B15 and other supplements touted as cures for ill-defined symptoms of "aging" are worthless; your money is more wisely invested in other areas of health maintenance.

The bottom-line of the vitamin business: If possible, get them from food; if not, consult your doctor.

ALCOHOL

It's called "the retirement disease." The sufferer may be a part of a fun-loving gang at an affluent retirement community, or a former high-powered executive trying to blot out empty days alone. They were once productive, but now, with nothing better to do, they use alcohol to lubricate their existence.

Alcohol is a substance that needs to be handled carefully, especially in retirement. Used in moderation, it can make us feel more sociable and fun-loving. Recent studies indicate moderate use may also cut risks of heart attack. But if use gets out of hand, alcohol the social catalyst quickly becomes alcohol the dangerous drug. As much as 10% of the retirement age population may abuse alcohol. Even those who've previously kept drinking well under control need to be careful. Abuse can start with the stresses of pretirement. Anxieties about the future, and unwillingness to let go of the past, can create pressure that alcohol temporarily eases. Then, retirement. No responsibilities. Freedom. And boredom. Unresolved transitional stress remains. There's certainly no shortage of potential drinking pals who are just as anxious as you are to party.

Enough can't be said about the negative impact and long-term dangers of excessive alcohol consumption. You don't have to get falling down drunk on a regular basis to suffer the negative effects of alcohol, particularly in the retirement age bracket. It interferes with nutrition, both by providing empty calories and by accelerating depletion of vitamins. It can cause depression, impotence, skin and digestive problems. It also impairs mental functions, suppresses immune responses, and adversely reacts with a host of medications commonly prescribed to the mature age group.

Be aware of your drinking habits during pretirement, and note any changes as retirement approaches. Analyze alcohol consumption as you did with food, noting where, when and why you drank each alcoholic beverage over the course of a week. Do an annual review of your drinking habits. Ideally, your drinking shouldn't increase in the latter stages of your career, and only moderately, if at all, during your post-career years. In some cases, it should decrease. When you have your medical exam, discuss your drinking patterns with your doctor. It's especially important to discuss this honestly because of the side effects alcohol may have on medication you're prescribed. If you have a problem with alcohol, willpower alone won't always be enough to see you through; counseling, therapy programs and medication can help reduce alcohol dependence.

Rules for Executive Alcohol Control Program

1. Monitor consumption patterns during your career.
2. Discuss your consumption frankly with your doctor.
3. Monitor consumption patterns during your post-career years.
4. Be aware of any increases in alcohol consumption during your career or after.

Sexuality

"Power is the ultimate aphrodisiac," Henry Kissinger observed, and many executives would agree. There's a feeling of virility and vitality that comes with a powerful position in an organization. Those you deal with acknowledge this in many subliminal ways. As retirement approaches, subconscious thoughts of losing this power, along with the thoughts of aging and fears about the future, can have an adverse impact on your sex life. This doesn't always mean a diminished sex drive; men and women in this position may engage in affairs as a way of convincing themselves of their continued desirability and vigor. Yet it may take as little as failure to achieve erection one night, combined with these other concerns, to produce a crisis of confidence in one's sexual desires and abilities.

There's no physiological reason for the onset of the middle years to signal the end, or even a downshifting, of sexual activity. There is a minor diminishing of sexual capabilities, but nothing that precludes an active and satisfying sex life for men or women. This is the fastest-changing area of the public's image of the mature individual. On TV and in the movies, the middle-aged and older are stealing the thunder from Hollywood's young hunks and starlets. There's nothing scandalous anymore about mature individuals leading healthy sex lives, and surveys indicate the majority of people between the ages of 60 and 65 continue to enjoy their sexuality.

HOW MUCH SEX SHOULD YOU BE HAVING?

While statistics and surveys dramatically show that sex can be an important and joyful part of life well into the advanced years, research doesn't indicate how much sex *you* should be having. If you've been sexually active throughout your life, plan on remaining that way. Conversely, if you haven't been sexually active, don't expect to retire to a life of lust. Major changes in sexual activity don't "just happen." But be aware of dramatic changes. They're not a normal part of aging, and if you experience them, look for the reason. Discuss the situation with your spouse, and your doctor or other specialist. Medication, as well as psychological factors, can affect the libido.

Couples should be aware of the minor physical changes both they and their partner may experience. This will prevent a sexual problem with a simple cause and remedy from creating a gulf of guilt, depression and marital strain.

Changes in Men
There's a gradual slowing of sexual response that accompanies aging. It takes longer to attain an erection, and sometimes it takes physical stimulation of the penis to become erect; hugging and kissing, or that certain look between couples may no longer be enough. In this case, impatience is the enemy of sexuality. On the plus side, the erection can be maintained longer before ejaculation. This means lovemaking can provide more pleasure.

Changes in Women
Women experience less decline in response. After menopause, decreased estrogen levels result in a thinning of the vaginal mucosa, possibly making intercourse painful for a woman. Unless couples

feel free to talk about this, he may feel neglected, and she may feel guilty. Estrogen treatments can help, but should be thoroughly discussed with a doctor due to potential dangers of hormone therapy. Even without hormone treatments, post-menopausal women can lead active sex lives.

It's your body and mind, and your life. It's within your ability, and certainly worth your while, to put effort into getting the most out of all three. Give the design, implementation and maintenance of your wellness program the emphasis it deserves, and you'll receive dividends compounded daily for many years.

P A R T V

EARLY
RETIREMENT

Sixty-five, as an age for retirement, is quickly becoming irrelevant. You've got to think in terms of when you want to retire, not when you must retire. The average age of retirement is currently 62, and it's edging downward. While executives tend to have longer careers than hourly wage earners, early retirement is still having a dramatic impact among the managerial ranks, and the impact will probably grow. A number of emerging trends and realities are responsible.

The Six Trends Accelerating Early Retirement

1. Liberalized pension plans and early retirement incentives
2. Business and management restructuring
3. Mergers and acquisitions
4. New attitudes about work
5. Desire for new challenge
6. Financial freedom

Liberalized pension plans and special early retirement incentives. Over 60% of the companies in one major survey now encourage early retirement as a matter of policy. This encouragement takes the form of pension provisions that provide unreduced benefits before the age of 65, or special "one time only" offers that many managers feel are too good to pass up. (These may be "one time only" in name alone; one airline offered this unique opportunity 11 times in five years.)

Vast retrenchment of businesses and management restructurings. Rapidly changing economic or work conditions cause some managers to retire before they would have, given more favorable business conditions. In corporate belt-tightening programs, executives may see perks trimmed, responsibilities drastically increased or decreased, or be faced with the necessity of relocating to maintain their jobs.

Mergers and acquisitions are eliminating many management positions. The increase in mergers and takeovers has led to an increase in the number and percentage of senior executives who depart soon after these "two for one" sales. A 1984 survey found almost half the executives queried looked for new jobs within a year of a merger, where only 20% had in 1981. Three-quarters of the 1984 respondents said they planned to leave within three years. In 1981, just over half responded that way.

Less stringent attitudes about the work ethic. Company loyalty isn't what it once was. The merger activity mentioned above has made many managers feel less dedicated to their careers. Many have friends and associates who've fallen victim to all the M&A action, and think, "There but for the grace of God go I." Additionally, a life of leisure is again considered respectable. This is especially true with the increase in semi-employment and other involving activities that can give shape to a life not centered around a career.

Desire for new challenge unsatisfied in current position. More executives are expanding their definitions of themselves, and looking for new career challenges beyond their present positions. For some, finances are a secondary consideration, and they retire early to pursue other areas of personal growth. For others, the chance to significantly increase their earnings through a business they start or become involved with provides the lure to early retirement.

Greater financial freedom makes continued employment unnecessary. Escalating compensation and greater sophistication in handling finances has removed financial pressure as a major employment factor for many maturing executives. For them, it's the sense of accomplishment and validation they get from a career that keeps them coming to work. If they find they're not getting this validation anymore, or can find it in a more satisfying activity, they can afford to pull up stakes.

Whether you're considering scripting your own exit, or wondering about accepting a newly announced and generous incentive package, the factors to consider are the same:

1. What are the advantages and disadvantages of continued employment versus early retirement?
2. What is motivating my desire to continue working?
3. What is motivating my desire for early retirement?
4. How complete are my plans for the future?
5. How thoroughly have I investigated early retirement?

Early Retirement: Three Executives' Experiences

The controller of a successful vacuum form packaging company decided to take advantage of his company's early retirement pension policy, put in his notice and left the company at age 56. Everything was fine. He enjoyed managing his investments, doing charity work and helping his son get his business started. Seven months after he left, his company offered an early retirement incentive that he would have been eligible for.

"I felt cheated," is how he described his feelings. He was bitter about it for over a year. "Eventually I realized I should be happy with what I do have, not with what I didn't get."

Another executive had considered early retirement, and concluded it was the right choice for him. Almost simultaneously, his company made a generous early retirement offer that affected hundreds of executives from mid-level managers up. Unfortunately, he was too valuable, and wasn't eligible. His solution?

"I'd decided that early retirement was right for me, so I retired early anyway." He didn't get the benefits and bonuses available, but he'd made the decision to move ahead already. There was no reason to hold himself back just because he wasn't getting what everybody else got.

A third executive found that the bonus made all the difference in the world. "I'd wanted to retire early and work with my wife. She'd started a consultancy, and I was going to join up with her. But looking at the numbers, we knew to do it right we'd need a little more capital to get things moving, and keep up our lifestyle. So I decided to keep working. When the company made their offer, I knew it was enough to make the difference."

There are two ways executives will come to consider early retirement. Either you, in a fit of foresight, will start mulling over this important question on your own (executive-initiated), or you'll suddenly be hit with an early retirement offer or unanticipated corporate shakeup that will force you to consider it (company-initiated). In the latter case, you may not be given as much time as you need to reach the right decision, one more reason why you've got to pre-plan the early retirement choice.

Unfortunately, questions about early retirement are much more likely to be provoked by an unexpected, company-initiated source, so we'll discuss them first.

CHAPTER THIRTEEN

COMPANY-INITIATED EARLY RETIREMENT

Company-initiated early retirement programs come in two varieties—official and unofficial. Official programs consist of ongoing early retirement benefits programs or "limited-time-only" early retirement incentive offers. Unofficial programs are generally the result of pressure, discrimination and job alteration or elimination.

Official Programs

Ongoing early retirement programs. These take a number of forms, and are applied in a variety of ways. Early retirement options might be part of company policy or part of an employment contract. In larger companies, the inducement may provide unreduced pension benefits and profit-sharing opportunities before the age of 65, or a liberalized actuarial reduction of the retirement discount; in other words, the pension is reduced somewhat to reflect a potentially longer payout, but not reduced to the extent dictated by actuarial tables.

If you're not sure exactly what your company's policy is, or the fine points of your contract, find out. If this kind of option is available to you, include this information in your pretirement planning. When you've drawn up the business plan for your future, you can plug these real numbers into your financial calculations, and see when you'll reach the financial targets that will allow you to put your plans into action.

Special early retirement incentives. These incentives, in one form or another, are now a part of the corporate landscape. From the top of the Fortune 500 on down, the preferred way to trim management ranks today is with an enticing incentive package. There may be lump sum payments, special stock options, appreciation rights, special dispositions of insurance plans. Golden parachutes flutter from the sky after takeovers and management changes. A third of the largest industrial companies offer their executives takeover protection in this form, making it very easy for them to bid a fond farewell instead of a bitter one.

These "official" early retirement inducements can sound very appealing. How do you know whether to take them or not? Before you decide, let's examine the factors that may interfere with objective decision making when faced with an unexpected early retirement offer.

THE GO, NO-GO DECISION

> ". . . Sometimes I have this gnawing fear that a number of people leave because of enticement, thinking they're going into a great and glorious land, and then find out later that they retired earlier than they should have from an emotional point of view."
> —Joseph Perkins, Corporate Retirement Manager, Polaroid Corporation

Early retirement is a business decision about your future. But many executives allow emotions to cloud their decision-making ability. The most common emotions are gratitude and rejection.

Almost opposite emotions, they can exist side by side when an executive responds to an unexpected early retirement offer. Such offers create a great deal of ambivalence, and this is reflected in the range of terminology used to describe the early retirement offer:

"Golden Handshakes"/"Golden Shoves" Often used simultaneously, as executives try to come to grips with extreme feelings that pull them in opposite directions. A combination of optimism and anger—an order masquerading as an offer.

"Open Windows" Ambivalence; indecisiveness. Is this a window from which one flies, or from which one falls, jumps or is pushed?

"Cordial Compulsion" Cynical, pessimistic, passive, resigned. An offer that can't be refused; the iron hand in the velvet glove.

A solid Company Man found himself adrift shortly after accepting an early retirement offer. "I didn't think about myself so much . . . The company had always been good to me, and I knew they were hurting. Besides, they made a generous offer."

Over and over, executives refer to "generous" offers. Companies don't make generous offers. They don't trot out early retirement bonuses, incentive programs and other inducements to be nice. They do it because they think it saves them money, or makes them more competitive. With changes sweeping over the economy and industry, a rapid pruning of the executive (and labor) ranks is often seen as the best coping strategy. Layoffs and firings create a negative impact. And younger employees need room to advance. So, the reasoning goes, why not offer an incentive to the most high-priced employees to leave, cutting payrolls and turning the reins over to younger and less expensive employees?

It doesn't always work out the way the company planned. The large cash outlays and hidden insurance and other costs the programs require make them expensive. Shifts in the business climate, and even within the company, can make the programs backfire. One mid-size manufacturing company offered an across-the-board retirement package to almost all salaried employees with more than 20 years of service. Over 40% of those eligible took advantage of it, and despite the cost, the company was going to save big money over the next five years. On paper, that is.

Shortly after the plan was put into effect productivity and quality control began slipping. Absentee rates climbed. Back-checking revealed the remaining managers were showing up just as often as they always had, but the attendance rate of the senior managers who'd left had been way above average, keeping the overall absentee figures at acceptable levels. As business picked up management found itself shorthanded, and younger executives didn't have the experience to pick up the slack. The result: The company began hiring back some of its furloughed execs as consultants at premium prices. Many of the best weren't available. They'd taken the bonus package and moved on to other jobs, knowing their skills and experience would be in demand. After adding up lost sales, orders that had to be reprocessed, missed opportunities and other unforeseen costs, the company felt lucky to break even on the deal.

While companies view early retirement as eliminating their most expensive employees, analysts and business consultants see it more akin to skimming the cream off the top, costing companies their most dependable, knowledgeable and dedicated employees. Any time you hear business analysts complain about the cost of these programs (complaints which, by the way, are growing quite loud), you know they must be potentially very advantageous for those who take them. And they are, *provided* you've done the proper research, analysis and planning, and find the program offered is consistent with your current situation and future goals.

A company is looking out for itself when it offers an early retirement incentive, and so should you when you consider it. Your job is to consider first whether early retirement in general makes sense for you, and, if so, whether a particular incentive program is the right one. Most companies can afford to make a mistake or cut a bad deal once in a while. With this once-in-a-lifetime business decision, you can't!

Feelings of rejection that arise in the wake of an early retirement offer are just as common and misplaced as feelings of gratitude. As the talk turns to how much the offer's worth, who's going to take it and who isn't, you can't help feeling hurt. Does this mean you and your colleagues haven't been doing a good job? Could it be that you're out of step with modern management? Does this mean they don't love you anymore?

Taking an early retirement offer personally is dangerous and ill-advised. It's impossible to make an objective decision if you feel the offer is a hidden message of obsolescence. If you're still not convinced, take a look at the way retirement programs are applied. They're typically across-the-board programs, open to all who meet the eligibility requirements. AT&T offered early retirement to 60,000 people at one time!

Few individuals have the power to alter the economy singlehandedly. Any manager who feels guilty and rejected, who thinks an across-the-board early retirement offer would never have been made if he'd just worked a little harder and made the bottom line a little blacker, is inflating his own importance. The result of this misguided thinking? If you feel obsolete, you'll act that way. Executives who would be better off remaining employed have left their company out of a sense of guilt. Others who can't or don't want to leave redouble their efforts and put tremendous pressure on themselves, though they're already doing a professional job. The potential cost to health, happiness and mental stability is great.

EARLY RETIREMENT VS. THE RETIREMENT TRANSITION

Early retirement may preclude the possibility of an orderly retirement transition. The offers set off cash register bells that drown out the emotional questions that need to be answered. Account for the negative emotions of retirement if you're leaving the work force ahead of schedule. It's vital for those who accept early retirement, particularly if they anticipate leaving the work force entirely, to implement an accelerated transitional program. Thoroughly working through the early retirement decision will get you through Realization and help you deal with the issues of Acceptance. Disengagement will still have to be negotiated, and it's not an easy process to accelerate. Plan compensating strategies for the potential problems caused by an incomplete transition. If you're responding to an early retirement incentive, take advantage of the support network that's about to be created around you. An early retirement offer usually means a large number of colleagues will vacate their positions. You may leave the office with an entire network intact, many of whom may face transitional problems. Attempts should be made to foster continuing formal and informal relations with these people if management personality and/or retirement inventories indicate a need for this contact.

WHY YOU HAVE TO CONSIDER AN OFFER BEFORE IT'S MADE

Well before the company grapevine carries the first hazy rumor of an impending retirement inducement, you should have considered it from all angles. When an offer is floated, you'll often have as little as two to four months to decide whether to accept it. That's not enough time to complete the analysis a major life decision needs. During your career, as you plan and execute an ongoing retirement transition, put an early retirement offer near the top of the list of the contingencies you plan for.

The particulars of an offer will play a major role in your reaction, but you need to know beforehand whether early retirement, in principle, is right for you. Can outside interests sustain you? Can you find other employment? Have you made realistic plans and worked out a post-career budget? At what point would a pension sweetener add enough to your income from investments to finance your plans? If you've answered these questions beforehand, you'll know what you need to make an early retirement offer acceptable. When and if an offer materializes, you can see if it has what you're looking for.

There's a flip side to this pre-offer planning. In companies without a rigid management structure it's possible for a manager to take the initiative in negotiating an early retirement package. This is especially true in smaller and family-owned businesses. If early retirement makes sense for you, and you know what would make it worthwhile, you may be able to make your own deal with the company, and work out an incentive package that has what you need.

THE EARLY RETIREMENT OFFER

> "There had been rumors floating around. The day they made the announcement, nothing got done. People gathered in small groups and talked about what they thought they'd do, but it was obvious nobody was prepared."
> —A manager, describing reaction to an unexpected early retirement offer.

Early retirement incentive packages are as varied as the thousands of companies that have offered them, but they usually incorporate common elements, a combination of pension bonus, insurance and health benefits, cash bonus and negotiables. The offer could come from a large, public organization, and leave little room for bargaining, or it could be from a smaller business or be aimed at an executive with an employment contract, and necessitate negotiating the entire package. Eligibility requirements also vary. A typical requirement might be 50 years of age and a minimum of 10 years with the company. The arithmetic can be pegged to a number representing a combination of age and years of service. If the number was 65, a 45-year-old with 20 years under the belt could exercise the early retirement option. The personnel department makes the final determination in individual cases. Valuable employees or individuals in understaffed departments may be ineligible. Seek outside, qualified help in understanding the financial and legal ramifications of any offers made to you.

Pension Bonus
Extra "phantom years" of service added to your pension. For example, five extra years may be figured into your benefits. If you've put in 17 years of employment, your pension will reflect 22 years.

Insurance and Health Benefits
The company may continue carrying you on the company life insurance program. They may continue your coverage on the company's medical and/or dental plan until Medicaid begins. Extension of death benefits may also be provided.

Cash Bonus
A lump sum severance payment. Typically, it's based on salary and tenure at the company. It may vary from a week's pay for every year of service to multiples of the annual salary. It may include a week's pay for every $10,000 of salary, or other adjustments. Sometimes, supplemental payments are offered until Social Security eligibility begins.

Negotiable Items
Negotiables are the most overlooked and least understood part of the early retirement incentive offer. Those who know what to ask for, and how to ask for it, can often arrange for benefits worth a great deal to them that cost their company very little.

Usually negotiables are carryovers of executive perks, or continuations of privileges available to current employees. Sometimes they're bonuses in the form of the company's goods or services. An airline threw in an item like this for everyone by offering free transportation for two on any flight for one year.

Catalog the perks and benefits you and other executives receive, and see which ones might be available to you on a continued basis. If your company maintains membership at a local country club, see if you can retain privileges. The same applies if your company has health facilities for employees.

If you feel you need free or low-cost office space for awhile, early retirement programs often mean a surplus of empty offices. Companies routinely provide office space to a dismissed executive to provide a temporary base of operations. Why shouldn't they do the same for an executive who leaves under more honorable circumstances?

Negotiate continued participation in company-sponsored social, sports and other activities if management personality and career history indicate that is necessary.

Don't fail to take advantage of negotiables in an early retirement offer. If you've planned right, you may be able to negotiate the points that spell the difference between an offer being acceptable and unacceptable. Making acceptance of an early retirement offer contingent on a few modest demands puts you in an excellent bargaining position.

There's one very important factor to keep in mind about early retirement offers: They are VOLUNTARY programs. This doesn't mean you won't feel pressured to leave in some cases. It means you can't let yourself be swayed by coercive attempts to get you to accept early retirement.

Unofficial Programs

We've talked about "official" early retirement programs. Now let's look at components of some not-so-official ones. Unofficial pressure is often a by-product of an official incentive program. Superficially, it's a voluntary program, and you've got two to four months to decide whether to take the offer and walk. But there's more to it than that. What happens if lukewarm response to the offer means the company's not saving as much money as they hoped? If you stay, what guarantee do you have that there won't be a layoff or firings down the line? The company isn't saying, and you're worried about passing up an attractive offer now, and being out on the street a little later. This is unofficial pressure.

This kind of pressure creates a tremendous amount of uncertainty and indecisiveness. Try to determine the level of acceptance the offer is meeting. The more people that accept the offer, the less pressure on those that stay. What's the outlook for the industry your company's in? How many people in the company duplicate your skills? Answering these questions will help you get a better idea of what the future holds, but even these efforts can fail you. Often, even top management doesn't know what lies ahead; they're waiting to see what happens with this early retirement offer just like you are. Then they'll decide what to do.

If you don't want to take the offer, start contingency planning based on a worst-case scenario. Pay close attention to your Business/ Employment Inventory. Think about and start laying the groundwork for other employment opportunities.

The future outlook at your company may be bleak enough to convince you to accept an early retirement offer you'd rather not accept. Use the inventory evaluations to identify areas to compensate for once you're no longer employed. Money and finances are usually a primary consideration, but don't lose sight of the others. The incentive may provide enough cash and/or pension enhancement to make a lower-paying job a viable alternative, greatly expanding the job market you can investigate.

Incentive offers create pressure from other sources, as well. Associates and colleagues who've accepted the offer may rib you about "workaholic" tendencies if you decide to stay. The teasing may lead you to question your decision. But this kidding masks the confusion and second guessing common to executives who've taken early retirement without proper planning. They're not sure they made the right choice, and the more people they see following their lead, the more comfortable and reassured they are. Your determination to keep working is seen subconsciously as undermining their decision. The last thing you want to do is base your decision on what "everyone else" is doing. Lemmings head off into the ocean en masse, but that doesn't mean it's good for all of them.

Younger employees may also exert subtle pressure. You may be viewed as an impediment to their own advancement. With the early retirement offer unveiled, their feelings may become more concrete and, as far as they're concerned, justified. "If they were pulling their weight, the company wouldn't be trying to get rid of them," is how one young hotshot put it.

Dealing with this pressure isn't as easy as sloughing off the mild barbs of retiring co-workers. This pressure is usually accompanied by increased power play activity among subordinates, as they jockey for the inside position on your job. Some may go so far as to run end arounds, bypassing you in the decision-making chain of command. In these situations, it's imperative that you remain productive, dynamic and in control. Gather your subordinates or the troublesome individual for an informal discussion. Spell out your plans, and what you expect from each of them in the future. If you have a role in designating individuals to carry on for you when you do retire, let them know that those who've been most productive and least disruptive will have a leg up on the competition. Additionally, personnel departments should make it clear to everyone that early retirement decisions are voluntary.

Sometimes there's more sinister pressure afoot. Stories are legion of executives who've been told they better accept an early retirement offer "or else." The courts are filled with lawsuits charging unfair dismissals, many lodged against top companies. Age discrimination complaints to the Equal Employment Opportunity Commission have been steadily climbing. They quadrupled between 1979 and 1983, and a good number can be traced to early retirement incentives.

Usually the coercive word is passed or insinuated by an immediate superior. He may be carrying out what he perceives as orders from above, or may try to turn a voluntary program into a compulsory one to make himself look good. He may think it's a feather in his cap if he can "persuade" subordinates to comply with voluntary cost-cutting measures, which is essentially what early retirement incentive programs are. A fine line separates legal from illegal pressure in these cases. There may be talk of increased workloads, evaporating perks, or somber hints of "big changes" ahead. Fault may be found with work that was always considered superior in the past. Or you may find yourself stuck with meaningless and unchallenging assignments.

If you are confronted with this problem, start with a frank discussion with your superior. Ask him to detail as explicitly as possible the changes he's been hinting at. Make notes afterward. Next, make an appointment with the director of human resources to further discuss the situation. In severe cases, it may require invoking your legal rights, and filing a discrimination complaint with the EEOC and/or a state employment rights agency.

PRESSURE WITHOUT THE OFFER

Early retirement pressure doesn't only accompany early retirement offers. Drastic restructuring of the work environment causes many executives to stop working earlier than they anticipated. One chemical company executive was informed the plant he'd worked at for most of his career in Buffalo was going to close. The company would guarantee him a job—if he was willing to move to Rochester. Another manager was told her job was going to be eliminated altogether. She could have a new job, but it would be at a reduced salary and have reduced responsibilities.

Many executives who've been terminated might envy these people; at least they have a chance to keep working. But those who face this kind of pressure often wish they'd been fired, so they wouldn't have to deal with the decision. It's a humbling and humiliating choice.

If you're faced with this situation, identify what you're working for. Money? Professional accomplishment? To give structure to your life? The inventories will help you identify the most important career components. Find out everything you can about the new position you're being offered. Which components will it provide? What is the future outlook? Is there a possibility that your responsibilities or pay will increase down the road? Could you be squeezed out altogether, a little bit at a time?

Companies that force these choices aren't naive. It's another way to reduce the payroll, and they usually put together an attractive severance package for those who aren't willing to trade down their jobs. Executives have more leeway to negotiate a benefits package in this situation than with across-the-board offers. Play your cards close to the vest. Ask lots of questions and don't give too many answers about your own intentions immediately. Put your deliberations on paper. Equally important are your alternatives. If you're unsatisfied with what you're being offered but want to keep working, what are your chances of finding a different job? If you already have well-formulated post-career plans, are they ready to be put into practice? If not, what needs to be done?

Getting another job is the most obvious alternative for those who aren't ready for early retirement. The best strategy is to hold onto your current job, even in a reduced capacity, while you begin putting out employment feelers and getting your resume in shape. This isn't always practical. If you're asked to relocate, you may decide it's not worth it. Make sure you formulate a rational rather than an emotional response.

TERMINATION

Being dismissed is a devastating psychological event. If you're over 50 and terminated, you wonder if this spells the end of your career. You need a solid plan for getting through this period of maximum stress.

Managers from top to bottom have been getting axed one way or another for a long time, and the action's been heating up lately. Often, the dismissals have no relation to professional performance. Mergers and takeovers leave a trail of pink slips. In the upper management ranks, personality conflicts and power plays can result in highly publicized sackings. Some terminations are sudden and unexpected, others can be seen coming. But all of them leave an executive feeling bitter and insecure. As depressing and earth-shattering as this event is, you can get through it, and go on to greater glory.

Dealing with Termination

No matter what your level in the management structure, or the reasons for your dismissal, job security issues should be handled the same way:

1. Keep your eyes open to warning signs.
2. If you're terminated, don't react emotionally.
3. Negotiate the best severance agreement you can.
4. Don't try hiding your termination from those close to you.
5. If you wish to be reemployed, mount a thorough and professional job search.
6. Don't accept a new job precipitously, out of desperation.

Keep your eyes open to warning signs. There are many signs pointing to potential trouble ahead. Poor performance ratings, clashes with superiors, and blown deals are the more obvious signs. But be aware of larger forces, as well. If your company is involved in a merger or acquisition, terminations are sure to occur. Assurances by your superiors are no guarantee. Promised job security can vanish in an instant. This "psychological contract" as one executive called it, is no longer inviolable. "I've had executives call me and say, 'I've lied to these people. I've double-crossed them. Can you come help me out?' The truth of the matter is that companies do lie," says one management consultant.

Even if you have a personnel file full of glowing reports, keep your eye on larger issues. Is your company being reorganized? Have there been any changes in the way your colleagues or superiors act toward you? Is a project you've been assigned leading to a dead end? If you have any reason to suspect your job's in jeopardy, have a frank talk with those you report to. In what direction do they perceive the company or your division to be heading? Do they anticipate changes? If you have reason to suspect your position isn't secure, start making contingency plans. This is especially true if your termination would be caused by a large reorganization. It's good to have a head start on a job hunt when many other executives may soon be joining you.

If you're terminated, don't react emotionally. No matter how unfair and unjustified you feel your termination is, *never* lose your temper or become abusive to whoever gives you the news, or whoever is responsible for the decision. Take the time to collect yourself. Postpone any discussion of severance or other important issues until you've had at least 48 hours to decompress and think things over. Giving in to feelings of frustration and hostility has only negative consequences. It diminishes you in the eyes of others, and it will diminish you in the eyes of yourself once you've had time to adjust to the shock.

Negotiate the best severance agreement you can. Severance agreements are usually open to negotiation. If you have a contract, the terms may be spelled out, but there may still be room for hammering out additional compensation. If you have no contract, the amount of money, insurance coverage, access to office space, and other perks may be negotiable. Consider what you think is fair, and write down a list of what you want. If you treat these negotiations in a businesslike manner, you have a much better chance of getting what you ask for. Companies don't like messy terminations any more than you do. They're often willing to try reaching an amicable settlement.

Don't try hiding your termination from those close to you. An executive with a large multinational financial services company rose to the head of European operations before coming back to work in the home office in New York. Shortly thereafter, he was terminated. The blow to his pride and dignity was devastating. For the next year, he got up and took the train in from Westchester like he always did, only instead of going to work, he looked for work. He never told his family he'd been dismissed. They learned about it a year later, when he had an emotional breakdown.

Being dismissed is a major trauma, and it's compounded when you keep it bottled up. It's important to vent your feelings, but not to your colleagues or superiors. You need the support of your family and friends. We can be very unforgiving and hard on ourselves, and at times like these we need the love and understanding of those we're close to, who can listen in a non-judgmental way. Share your feelings with people you feel comfortable with. If not family or friends, then a therapist or psychologist. Left inside, your pain will grow and consume you from within, crippling your ability to move ahead.

If you wish to be reemployed, mount a thorough and professional job search. The higher the fall from the executive ladder, the more time and dedication it takes to regain a similar perch. Use all the tools at your disposal. More companies are providing outplacement services to their terminated employees. By one estimate, three times more companies now offer outplacement programs as did in 1980. Anybody or any organization involved in your job search is an assistant. It is your responsibility to work with them, and use their expertise and contacts to get you into a position to sell yourself.

Your relationship with the outplacement counselor is important. You're going through a rough time, and need both professional guidance and a supportive individual who has your best interests at heart. This isn't what you always get. Outplacement companies can be serving three different interests besides their own simultaneously. Most visibly, they help you. But they're paid by your company, whose best interests are perceived as your quick reemployment, even if the available job isn't quite right for you. Some outplacement firms also act as headhunters, in which case the needs of the organization you are being placed in also have to be served. Sometimes all these interests coincide, other times they don't. Be aware of what your interests are, and what you're looking for when you deal with any outplacement, referral, headhunting or other placement firm.

Use your industry resources and contacts as well. Put out the word about your availability. Your job search has to be customized to the position you are looking for. At higher levels, sending out resumes blind is a mistake. Follow up leads with a telephone call first. Try to speak to those who are in a position to do the hiring. Don't bad-mouth your former employer. Be honest about your termination and enthusiastic about your abilities. It can take from several months to over a year to find an equivalent position. Don't get discouraged. Finding the right employment situation is a full-time job.

Don't accept a new job precipitously, out of desperation. Be extremely careful about accepting a job offer. It's similar to love on the rebound—there's a tendency to grab at the first thing that comes along. Don't take any job that's offered just to convince yourself that your skills are still in demand. It can be hard to turn down a job when you've been searching for a few months, even when something not quite right presents itself. Ask yourself if this is a position you would have taken had you not been terminated. In the final analysis, it's a judgment call on your part, but keep in mind the temptation to accept the unacceptable just to have a job. That approach isn't fair to you, and it's not fair to the organization that wants to hire you.

CHAPTER FOURTEEN

EXECUTIVE-INITIATED EARLY RETIREMENT

Many executives are no longer waiting for a company incentive plan to plunge into the future. They look forthrightly at the options in their careers and out of it, and choose to go their own way. Their early-retirement decisions may be a prelude to a second career, or a conscious decision to lead a more relaxed lifestyle. Their decisions may be precipitated by a career disappointment, like being passed over for a key promotion, or by a desire for greater challenge. Newspaper and magazine business sections are filled with such stories. "I had always said that if I didn't get to head the broadcast group by the time I was 55 I would leave, and I gave it an extra year. My feeling is I very much want to have a chance to do something for me, and I've got 10 more years to really enjoy life as an entrepreneur," says a former network executive. "My wife and I just have a lot of other things that we want to do in our lives while we still enjoy good health. We're very deeply committed to our church involvements, and I've got a lot of outside interests in community affairs, including the Boy Scouts and the United Way," says a drug company president about his early retirement decision.

A former vice president of a training company took early retirement and founded a successful office automation consultancy. "It was not difficult at all because I had an expertise that through my networks was well known and was needed," she says.

If you feel your current career has reached a dead end, early retirement may be a way out. Consider what you're looking for. Do you want to work in a new or related field? Are you looking for a position where you'll be able to advance to the top, or for a less-pressured environment? Do you want to run your own business? This last option is one more executives are choosing after early retirement. One headhunter estimates 10% of the executives she counsels now go into business for themselves, up from 2% at the beginning of the decade.

The generous severance packages that early retirees can negotiate give them the financial freedom to pick and choose the opportunities that suit them best. Put time and effort into deciding your course. One executive couple spent two years traveling the country and talking to local Chambers of Commerce and businesspeople about opportunities before they found the right one—a small printing company in northern Florida that's making a profit on sales of about five million dollars a year.

Consideration and preparation for early retirement needs to be, perhaps, even more thorough than for traditional retirement; you'll have more time to regret a wrong decision, and you're tossing away a valuable investment of time in your present career before it has really paid off. The three Ps—pay, perks and pension—really start getting sweeter during the last decade of an executive's career.

The problem is that an executive considering early retirement doesn't have the same options in preparing for it as he might for traditional retirement. Many of the avenues for experimenting with a new lifestyle may be unavailable. You won't find colleagues and top brass as understanding of attempts to implement a phasing program or retirement rehearsal. Moreover, most top-flight managers who retire early feel an overriding sense of mission to become more involved with their work, partly owing to feelings of guilt for leaving friends and colleagues to carry on without them. Once they make the decision to leave, many early retirees become virtual fixtures at the office, in an attempt to get things in order—as though they were dying, instead of preparing for a new life.

Work after Early Retirement

"Hiring older managers has become much more acceptable. In the next ten years older people will be working longer. This is the beginning of a trend. Middle-aged persons can teach younger managers. I think it is not much more difficult for them to get jobs."
—Clifford J. Benfield, President, Hay Career Consultants

For many executives early retirement signals the start of a new career. If you're wondering what possibilities there are for you, the answer is "plenty."

The stereotypes of middle-aged managers as unwanted job applicants is quickly disappearing. Outplacement companies report a growing trend to hire the 50+ manager. One placement firm recently found that for the first time, they were placing managers over 50 in jobs faster than those under 50, and the trend held through three of the four quarters of the year.

It's not surprising. The mature manager has solid credentials, long work experience, is generally more dependable, less likely to be hired away, and adds a small burden to company pension plans.

Some execs who don't want to stop working, but feel an early retirement offer is too good to pass up, look for lateral employment opportunities. They move into positions similar to the one they just vacated. If this is what you have in mind, check with the personnel department before plunging ahead. Some companies forbid former employees to work for competitors. Anyone who "defects" will be jeopardizing their early retirement bonus and benefits package. Check with your industry contacts, too. One V.P. of a shipping company had been fending off feelers from a competitor for several years. He accepted an early retirement offer thinking he'd have no trouble finding a similar job. But the same pressures that forced his company to float the incentive were felt by their competitors, and his specialized skills weren't in as much demand as he thought.

What If I Made a Mistake?

Some former managers may be reading this a little late. Perhaps they're scanning through this chapter to see what they *should* have done before they took the plunge and accepted an early retirement offer several weeks or months ago. Some are convinced they made the wrong choice, and don't know what to do about it.

Don't automatically assume that an initial unhappy retirement experience means you made the wrong choice. A career may shield an executive from troubling issues in his domestic or personal life. With the shield removed, he comes face to face with a source of conflict and unhappiness. Longing for the career, in this case, is a self-directed ruse that actually stands in the way of future growth and happiness.

Objectively analyze your feelings of unhappiness or anxiety to determine their source. The inventories can help you isolate areas that are causing problems, either by revealing a deficit of alternative activities, or identifying areas of conflict in your personal life. If the inventories lead you to conclude lack of employment really is at the root of your problems, identify the components of your former position you miss the most. Was it the routine of a daily schedule? Feelings of productivity? A paycheck that served as a tangible reminder of your worth? The social interactions of the office? By identifying the components, you can devise compensatory strategies that can provide the same positive feedback. A young retiree from an industrial container manufacturer set up a daily schedule that got him out of his house by 10 a.m. four days a week. Another former manager plunged into a heavy commitment with social and volunteer organizations to meet his socialization needs. A third undertook marriage counseling with his spouse, realizing that the problems his career had helped hide could no longer be avoided.

If, after careful consideration, you are still convinced that only a return to your former position can restore your happiness, your options are more limited. Marching back in and asking for your old job has met with minimal success ever since Napoleon returned from Elba. However, a growing number of companies are hiring former employees on an "as needed" basis, though more often hourly rather than salaried employees. Get in touch with the personnel department and find out the part-time hiring policy. If there are no clear guidelines, you might point out that it's cheaper to hire employees who already know the job, instead of training new ones. If you haven't accepted an early retirement offer yet, make it a point to inquire about part-time employment possibilities before you do check out.

Remember, unhappiness following early retirement acceptance doesn't mean you made the wrong choice. Don't limit your options to your present post-career lifestyle and your former career-oriented one. There are many other ways to travel the road to future happiness, and you need to keep an open mind in exploring them all.

PART VI

AFTER RETIREMENT

Y ou've said your last goodbyes at the office, been toasted and roasted, finished hashing over old times with colleagues, and now retirement is really here. For a few days or weeks, you may be stumbling around trying to get your bearings.

The First Few Days

It's fine to set aside a period simply to get acclimated to your new surroundings. The last few weeks may have been hectic, and you may want to relax, sleep late and just enjoy the quiet of your home. Knowing you have a plan of action to implement after this breather will allow you to enjoy it, instead of being anxious and stressed by lack of a future objective.

This is an excellent time for reviewing the plans you've made for your future. Discussing them with your spouse or other involved individuals in this unpressured environment is the post-career equivalent of the executive retreat, where you may have huddled with other managers to formulate long-range policy, or review progress in a relaxed setting. Schedule sessions in the morning or afternoon of at least two days within this period to discuss the plans you've drawn up, and your implementation programs. Be prepared to make a statement, marking the significance of the arrival of the event you've been preparing for. It's an upbeat occasion. Make sure your remarks reflect this.

THE FIRST MONDAY

Make the first Monday of retirement a special day. Plan on doing something you will enjoy, that transmits the message you are beginning a new life. One suburban executive and her husband spent a luxury weekend at a hotel in New York City. On Monday morning they got up and went to the heliport for a chartered copter ride around the city, something she'd always talked about doing. Another executive had a catering company come to the house and prepare a lavish brunch for his wife and him. A third bought books and records.

Start off with a positive and enjoyable activity. Send a message to yourself, of the benefits and possibilities of retirement, and immediately put those possibilities into practice.

THE POST-CAREER VACATION

Vacations follow retirement with almost the same regularity that day follows night. The vacation provides a chance to relax, a tangible reward for the completion of a career, a period of celebration before the day-to-day, post-career life begins. Many executives sabotage their chances for a successful getaway by having ill-defined plans, inadequate preparations or unrealistic expectations. This causes two problems. The vacation is unsatisfactory and the new retiree returns with a bitter taste from his first post-career project, prompting a dour view of post-career life.

If you're married communication with your spouse is essential. Many vacations have been ruined before they got started because one-half of the couple expected a relaxed agenda, and the other half wanted to see everything.

You've got plenty of time to go on vacations from now on. Don't overextend yourself on this first one, trying to make it into an all-inclusive trip, to see all the sights you've been waiting years to see, *and* to relax. The more ambitious your travel plans, the longer the period of time between the last day of your job and the first of your vacation. If all you want to do is lie on the beach for a few days, you could be on the plane the day after you leave work. But you'll enjoy extended trips much more if you take time to really get ready for them.

If you're planning on spending a month in Europe, or anywhere else, put time into research. Go to the library and read up on the spots you plan to visit. Get in touch with the government tourist boards. Learn about seasonal events. This kind of planning will make your trip much more rewarding, and you'll find the planning adds an element of excitement and anticipation you'd never experience if you just left arrangements up to a travel agent and got on a plane or a cruise ship.

Separation: The Final Transitional Stage

After the heady decompression period surrounding the date of retirement is over, the work of Separation begins. It's the last stage of the retirement transition, and has no counterpart in the office environment. Some executives sail right through. For others, Separation is the most troublesome stage of all. No matter who you are, and what your agenda is, your goals for Separation are as follows:

- Terminate dependence on former career.
- Aggressively implement post-career plans.
- Adjust to post-career lifestyle.
- Monitor and modify post-career plans as necessary.

Terminate Dependence on Former Career
Your first order of business is getting over feelings of loss of career. There's a temptation to spend time wondering what they're doing back at the office, or how your successor is making out. Retirement still seems like a strange land, and your natural impulse will be to grab for something stable. At this point, your former career represents the zenith of stability in your universe, so you continue trying to hold onto it. Unless you terminate this dependence, you'll remain mired in the past.

Aggressively Implement Post-career Plan
If you've handled your transition properly, you've invested time and effort into planning your future. You've discussed an agenda with your spouse and family, and taken active steps to "rehearse" your future. Now's the time to roll up your sleeves and put these plans into action. Having a positive forward direction to move in will keep you from looking backward.

Adjust to Post-career Lifestyle
You may have an agenda brimming with things to do, or you may have a more leisurely lifestyle planned. Whatever your goals, you

should realize retirement has a different pace, a different ethos. It can take a little getting used to after a hectic career. You must learn to be relaxed in pursuing your post-career goals, and comfortable with your new identity.

Monitor and Modify Post-career Plans as Necessary

No matter how well prepared you are, there will be surprises ahead. Things never work out exactly as planned. Be prepared to alter and modify your plans to meet changing situations, or changing goals, down the road. The mature years are perhaps less static than any other time of life, and require more adjustment than any other period. If you're prepared to fine-tune or alter your plans, you'll see it as a challenge, not a bothersome and daunting task.

SEPARATION EXERCISES

1. Arrange a social gathering with the stipulation that no one discuss work or business.
2. Attend a meeting of any kind of group of retired executives.
3. Make a list of five or more positive things you are able to do in retirement that you weren't able to do in your career.
4. Make a list of your accomplishments thus far in retirement.

During Separation, make no effort to contact anyone from your organization, unless you've made previous plans to participate in a company alumni or retiree group. The testimonials, parties and other retirement activities gave you and your colleagues a chance to say goodbye. There's no healthy reason for saying hello again so soon.

Start developing your post-career social network. Look up any of the retired individuals you spoke to during Pretirement. Get together with them for lunch or any other suitable occasion. Fill them in on your plans, and solicit feedback from them.

I Miss My Career . . . I Think

It's impossible not to think about your old job, the office, what the gang's up to. The thoughts range from brief reflection to abject longing. Let's examine the latter case. Robert Zimmer hasn't been very happy with his retirement for the first six months. More and more, he thinks about his career. He had some vague plans to pursue in retirement, but his continued identification with his career has kept him from implementing his plans. The less adjusted he feels, the more he wishes he was still working.

Yes, Robert does have a problem; it's his oversimplified way of looking at his past, present and future. He's creating an either/or situation that's impossible to resolve. It's either the life of his former career, which he can't have back, or the unsatisfying lifestyle he's now leading. What Robert isn't seeing is the wealth of opportunities that surround him. Because he's not happy with the course he's set for himself, or the drifting feeling he gets from having no definite direction, he identifies his unhappiness with "missing" his career. He's forgotten the choice isn't between retirement and career, the choice is among all the opportunities and possibilities of the post-career years.

Post-career adversity isn't the signal to put your tail between your legs and dream of scampering back to the warmth and reassurance of your office. If you're having trouble overcoming your career dependence, write a list of what it is you miss; divide the list into the categories of "Career General" and "Job Specific." Typical listings would be:

Career General	*Job Specific*
Feelings of productivity	Friends at work
Paycheck	Company credit card
Interaction with others	Specific perks
Position of leadership	Particular project
Chance to exercise skills	Limousine service

Next, list what it is about your present lifestyle you're not enjoying. Be specific. Avoid looking at it as an ill-defined, vague malaise. Here are typical sources of post-career unhappiness:

1. My spouse and I aren't getting along.
2. I don't have enough friends.
3. I'm not involved in many social activities.
4. My plans are too demanding.
5. My current agenda is too unchallenging.
6. I don't like the climate where we moved to.
7. I'm worried about the cost of maintaining our lifestyle.

Being specific about the causes of your feelings puts you on the path to turning things around. When Robert Zimmer made his lists, he identified the interaction with people as one of the *general career components* he missed most. He had also had close friendships with associates, developed during his 17 years with the company, and listed that as a *job specific component* of his career he missed. As for his current lifestyle, he realized he didn't have many social connections in the Sunbelt community he and his wife had moved to. And the European cruise they'd planned was making him worry about other expenditures down the road, whether they'd have enough money to indulge themselves the way they wanted.

With the problem defined, a plan of action can be developed. Robert made a list of social and civic organizations in the community, and began investigating them to find groups he'd enjoy being a part of. Discussions with his accountant allayed fears about going broke, but at the same time reinforced the importance of budgetary restraint to both him and his wife. He also invited a former colleague to spend a week visiting them. Six months later he had begun putting his post-career life on a firm foundation, and was no longer thinking wistfully about his former job.

Warning Signs of Incomplete Separation

Some executives never complete Separation. Their post-career years are marked by intense longing for the past. Among the indications that Separation is incomplete:

1. Excessive attempts to maintain social ties with former colleagues.
2. Ongoing interest in the inner machinations at your former company.
3. Excessive reference to your former position in conversations and at social gatherings.
4. Preoccupation with old career setbacks and/or disappointments.
5. Finding excuses to drop by or call the office.
6. Continuing to define yourself internally by your former position.

Executives in this situation need to take an aggressive approach to turning things around. Potential courses of effective action include employment, involvement in a support or therapy group, and intensive development of a hobby or other interest in a group situation. Forcing yourself out of the house to play golf or attend a social function isn't going to be enough to snap you out of your doldrums.

After Separation

The Separation phase of retirement typically lasts between six and 18 months. Gradually you'll think less about the past and more about the future. You'll have an agenda that suits you, and be involved in the business of your life. You'll look back on your career and think not of a parade that's marched on and left you behind, but of a fork in the road where you moved in one direction, and those you worked with moved in another.

The completion of Separation marks the end of the challenges of your career transition. Look back at the four objectives of Separation, and judge for yourself whether you've successfully completed them. You're not home free, yet. This is really the beginning of the challenges of post-career life. With career transition issues behind you, you can devote full energies to exploring new options and opportunities, and refining your management of the business of your life. Minimizing the job ahead would be like thinking an executive could sit back and watch the profits roll in once a company was incorporated. Getting operations on-line means the challenges are just beginning. So too in retirement. Continue to challenge yourself. Keep asking yourself if you are getting as much out of your life as you want, if you are performing at your optimum level.

I WANT TO ENJOY RETIREMENT, NOT "WORK" AT ENJOYING IT

For the well-adjusted individual, the work of creating an enjoyable retirement won't be difficult. After Separation, as you fine-tune post-career plans, you'll hone your strategy so that the business of your life practically runs itself. It will still require oversight and periodic reviews, to ensure things are operating smoothly. But once you've set your course and are satisfied with the direction, you can switch on the autopilot and concentrate on enjoying your lifestyle, be it in a second career or in a hammock. We can't sugarcoat the challenges faced by executives who aren't adjusting well to retirement; those who find themselves bored, unhappy, putting on weight, depressed, directionless. These individuals have two choices: They can continue in their downward spiral, or they can roll up their sleeves and really work at becoming successful (using either the guidelines in this book or any other method they find effective). Make no mistake, it's not an easy job, but it's a vitally important one, and you're the only person in the world who can handle it.

No matter how well or poorly you are adjusting to your post-career life, there are a number of avenues of opportunity you should keep in mind to make your job easier. Be ready to take advantage of them.

Networking

This isn't only for the upwardly mobile. Networking is the process of establishing mutually supportive and beneficial contacts. As a retiree you have many networking opportunities, because of the time you can invest in establishing and taking advantage of these contacts, and because of the number of organizations geared specifically to individuals like you. There are many groups run by and for retired executives. They can provide opportunities to exercise your executive skills, and social networks of kindred spirits you can turn to for friendship and moral support. Organizations ranging from the American Association of Retired Persons to SCORE, the National Executive Service Corps, and others, offer opportunities for retired executives to meet and use their skills constructively. Civic and community groups are also a good place to find people who may have lots in common with you. Don't neglect to cultivate your friendships. Having friends can provide one of the most valuable support networks at any age. Don't expect more from others than what you're willing to put into cultivating and maintaining relationships. Host a dinner or cocktail party. Invite friends over for bridge or to watch a movie. Stay involved with people. Avoid becoming isolated.

Volunteer Activities

Volunteer and charity work is the most common suggestion for how an executive can occupy himself in retirement, and there's good reason. There are thousands of organizations that need you.

Some need your knowledge and skills, other equally worthy organizations need people whether they have executive skills or not. Retirees can provide a helping hand.

Volunteer work fulfills a number of needs:

- Socialization: It keeps you involved with people.
- Productivity: It helps you feel needed and appreciated.
- Altruism: It provides a positive feeling of returning to society some of what you've earned from it.
- Mental stimulation: Being turned loose on a new set of challenges keeps you mentally active.
- Imposes structure on your schedule: The value of having blocks of time around which a day can be structured can't be underestimated.
- Promotes post-career business interests: For an executive embarking on a second career, the right organizational involvement can prove invaluable in furthering post-career plans and making valuable contacts.

Volunteer work can be tremendously fulfilling. It can also leave you feeling bored, uninvolved and in a make-work situation. In order for the arrangement to benefit both the organization and the volunteer, you have to choose the kind of work, and the organization itself, carefully. Ask yourself which of the above-mentioned benefits are most important to you. Look for the group that will provide them in an environment you feel comfortable in.

Visit various groups in your area, and look for ones that most closely mesh with your management philosophy and methods of operation. If you only want to expand your social circle, look for a group whose members you get along with. Do you want to contribute time to a worthy cause? The group must be involved with something you really believe in and are willing to devote time to. Do you want to exercise particular management skills? Make sure the organization has room for your input, and that the kind of position you'd like to occupy isn't already taken.

Finding the right organization to devote your time to should be as carefully considered as finding the right job. Contact organizations and find out their programs. Contact local government officials, and find out what programs they support or what problems they see in the community.

Go to the white pages of the phone book, and look under headings that start with the words "American," "National," and "United." Besides airlines and commercial businesses, you'll find nonprofit organizations and volunteer groups. The range of listings will trigger more ideas on what kind of groups you might like to work with.

Don't limit yourself. You don't have to work with an established group. You can start your own. One executive, concerned about the deteriorating quality of a small neighborhood park, started doing yard work in it. Her involvement got other people interested. Soon she had a local plant store contributing shrubbery and was overseeing a coalition of neighborhood people helping to improve the park. From there she set her sights on other community problems, and became active in community politics.

Retraining

Employment can provide the involvement and feeling of productivity many executives miss the most. But your skills may not match the available opportunities. Maybe there isn't a great demand for your expertise where you relocated. But courses offered by technical schools or other outlets can teach you new skills. Whatever skills you learn, make sure they are something you enjoy doing, not something you are intent on making money at.

Keep your definition of retraining flexible. Sometimes you can get paid to do it. Feeling too inactive after moving to Orlando, a retired executive got a part-time job as a computer operator, even though he had no idea how to run the equipment; they gave him on-the-job training. He was no computer hacker, but the skills were fairly simple to learn, and made him feel like he was on the cutting edge of technology. Now he works whenever he feels like it, but more importantly, he took his newfound interest home, and now has a personal computer he uses for tracking investments, writing letters, and playing computer games when his grandson comes to visit.

Don't limit yourself to possible employment as the sole reason for retraining. Allocate a portion of your educational budget for pursuit of hobbies and interests.

Learning Opportunities

Adult education is growing by leaps and bounds. Learning has become a lifelong activity. Education can be a lot more fun when you have the freedom to pursue knowledge without the pressure to put it to use. Formalized learning opportunities are available through college courses, community learning networks and private instruction. Don't be constrained by classrooms and instructors. You can create your own opportunities to learn more about things you're interested in. There are clubs and societies devoted to particular interests. Libraries are stocked with information.

If you're interested in French Impressionism, don't stop after registering for an art appreciation course of drawing lessons. Call up the curator of your local museum, invite him or her to lunch, and discuss your interest. Find out the names of others who are interested in the subject. Develop an informal discussion group. Plan trips to nearby galleries, or even the Louvre. Keep your mind open to new opportunities.

Temporary and Part-time Work

For those who don't want the level of involvement demanded by a second career or intensive volunteer work, temporary or part-time employment is a viable alternative for keeping active. As you may know from experience, temporary work is mushrooming as corporations slim down. Core employees are augmented by an army of temporaries. It's a seller's market. Many temp agencies now offer training for part-time workers. Skills one formerly paid to learn in business courses or secretarial schools are now often provided gratis. The newly computerized ex-manager mentioned above is an example of this trend.

The built-in flexibility of temporary work is one of its greatest assets. Devote as much or as little time to it as you want. The structure, learning and socialization are its major benefits. Look at the paycheck as a bonus. Call local temporary agencies and get information about them. Ask to speak to some of the temps, and drop by their offices.

Temporary agencies don't have the part-time job market locked up. There are opportunities all around you, and they are growing all the time. From fast food to clerical work, jobs are going begging, and the people being begged to step in are your age. In the late 1970s, 3 million people a year entered the labor market. By the early 1990s, the figure will drop to around 1.3 million, as the baby bust generation reaches its majority. Hundreds of thousands of service jobs that used to be filled by teenagers will be taken over by maturing Americans. Often, these employment opportunities can bolster or reinforce current interests. One former mid-level manager who loved books and reading found himself a part-time job in a bookstore. Another who fancied herself an amateur gourmet chef got a job in a gourmet food shop. These aren't necessarily the post-retirement jobs all executives are looking for, but they're nonetheless solid opportunities for involvement, socialization and spare change.

Support Groups

A variety of support groups, from formal to loosely structured, offer help and camaraderie to those who feel estranged or alone. People come to meetings to talk over their thoughts and problems. They gain insight by expressing their feelings and hearing how others respond. Learning how other people dealt with difficult situations can help you see solutions and get a perspective on your own problems. Focus on what kind of support you're looking for, and then seek a group that can provide it. Groups may be aimed at specific problems, like drinking or smoking, or have a much more open-ended agenda. They may include people of various ages, or be limited to a specific bracket. Groups may be large or small. Some may have a professional as a moderator and have a regular group of participants. Others are run by an ever-changing cast of participants. If you're trying to work through problems, it's usually best to be involved in a group that encourages positive efforts, rather than one that mainly serves as a forum for airing unhappiness. Departments of Public Health, religious organizations, doctors and therapists can supply information about various groups. If possible, try out a few of those that seem most promising.

Therapy

Don't try biting the bullet and plunging ahead on your own if you have trouble coping with your problems. Get professional help. Sometimes it takes therapy to impose goals and provide direction from the outside. A therapist with knowledge about your background, strengths and weaknesses, can help you devise the right program. Watch for these warning signs that signal a need for therapy:

- Rapid gain or loss of weight
- Serious marital discord

- Inability to adjust to retirement
- Continued depression
- Suicidal thoughts

Consulting your physician is the first step. Your problems may be the result of a physical disease process, or a side effect of medication you've been prescribed. If the examination finds nothing physically wrong with you, your physician can recommend professional therapists and programs. Look for someone who's worked with retirement-age individuals before. The right therapy program will help you get in touch with your feelings and help you define realistic short- and long-term goals. The act of seeking therapy is extremely positive; it shows you're aware of problems, and willing to take concrete steps to correct them.

Those reluctant to get help should ask themselves why. Is it the social stigma? Embarrassment? You're not sure whether you really need help? Do you have the John Wayne syndrome, thinking only sissies need help? A Superwoman complex? Focusing on the reasons you are not taking advantage of available assistance will help you break down your resistance to getting it. There's no sin in needing help, but there is in avoiding it.

Corporate Alumni Groups and Retiree Clubs

If you're unable to completely separate from career, and unable to remain employed, the support and sense of belonging provided by a corporate alumni group or retiree club can help. Companies like General Electric, Xerox, Time, Inc., and McKinsey have spawned such groups. AT&T has a longstanding alumni group for retirees. These organizations are loosely organized, and the degree of official corporate support varies. They sponsor trips, publish newsletters, and hold more-or-less annual meetings. Some publish directories of members, assisting in establishing social contacts with kindred spirits in your area.

Don't plan on getting overly involved with an alumni group or retirement club; it can keep you focused on the past. But if you really can't get the company out of your system (an extreme Company Man tendency), plunge into it. If your last company doesn't have an organization like this, see if any of the other companies you've worked for do. Maybe others miss the camaraderie as much as you do. Look into getting a group started. Few companies with these programs would have them if brave alumni hadn't organized them.

Post-career Housing

Thinking of moving? There are many excellent reasons for relocating, but there are also excellent reasons for advising you never to relocate during Separation. There are exceptions to every rule, but in general moving to another home or city within the first year of retirement or before Separation is complete can be a strategic error. Retirement alone makes the top ten in stress-producing life situations. Relocating is another major stressor, and while it's lower on the list, stressful situations have a cumulative effect.

Waiting to relocate will help you gauge your post-career adjustment. The standard of satisfaction and happiness you enjoyed during your career can be used as a baseline with which to compare your feelings about retirement. If you relocate, you'll be bombarded by new stimuli, and it'll be difficult to know what's causing adjustment problems. Is it your new home, your new social surroundings or your newly retired status? In familiar surroundings, it's much easier to keep tabs on post-career changes in attitude and outlook.

The perspective you get on the city you live in is much different when seen from retirement than when seen from career. Waiting to move gives you an opportunity to see your community in a new light. It could be that it has a wealth of organizations, facilities and opportunities you never had the time to find out about while you were busy climbing to the top. You should be thoroughly familiar with your present surroundings, and what you like and don't like about them, before you relocate.

There are more reasons for postponing relocation. The decision to move may be a knee-jerk reaction to inactivity or an unstructured retirement. This is one of the poorest possible reasons for moving. Relocation should be born of a desire to go "to" someplace, not escape "from" someplace or something.

This brings us to the subject of exceptions to the rule. Here's one: A dentist, with a thriving practice in Chicago, and his wife loved skiing and the outdoors. In particular, they loved Aspen, and spent as much time there as they could, skiing in winter, taking advantage of the cultural activities in the summer. A large windfall his wife received made them sit down and take stock of their future, and what they really wanted to do. The upshot: He sold his practice, they moved to Aspen, built a house and have lived happily ever since.

If you think you're an exception to the rule, write a list of the factors influencing your decision, and see if they're strong enough to overcome the reasons for avoiding a quick relocation. Look back over the section on Housing in Chapter 9. If you're planning on making a rapid, permanent move you must be:

1. Thoroughly familiar with the place you are moving to
2. Financially able to make the move and maintain the lifestyle you want to lead, and able to make another move if this one doesn't work out

When and if you do relocate, keep in mind the various living arrangements available. Do you want to live in an adult community where there will be less diversity in people, but more common interests? Do you want to go condo, and lessen the amount of upkeep you'll be responsible for? You may decide to make intermediate moves. One couple moved to Florida, and got a house on the water where they tied up a boat. They felt it would be fun enjoying the water and the property for a few years, but ›2anticipated›1 they'd later want to move to a club community or condo where they wouldn't have to worry about maintenance. Don't feel stuck somewhere once you've made a move.

VACATION HOMES

Whether retirement qualifies as a permanent vacation or not, you may not want to live in the same place year round. Don't feel you have to. If you find summers in the Sunbelt too hot, think about putting in a few months farther north when the thermometer starts rising. A change of scenery will keep you from getting too bored with your primary residence, and reinforce your freedom to experiment with different lifestyles.

Ask retirees who've moved south what their biggest adjustment was, and a surprising number answer the lack of seasons. "Up north, you see the seasons change, it gets cold and then hot, and even though you bitch about the weather, at least you know things are changing. Here it's always the same," said one former exec surveying the ocean from his porch in Florida.

Having a place to get away to, whether for a season or for a few weeks a year, can help you avoid the feeling of stagnation, no matter what part of the country you live in.

Travel

Planning travel can be exciting and fun. Making the arrangements is often a different story. Executives aren't used to dealing with the ins and outs of reservations, checking for discount flights and accommodations, or hunting for travel bargains. If you've got to be in Houston for an important meeting at 10:30 tomorrow morning, your secretary makes the arrangements, and tells you your flight number and what time to be at the airport. Who cares what the ticket costs? But in retirement you've got to take an active hand in travel arrangements.

You'll find out what your secretary and the corporate travel office have known all along: Fares and schedules are a byzantine labyrinth of confusing tariffs, restrictions and prices. And now you're picking up the tab instead of the company. You don't have the expense account anymore, but you have things that are almost as valuable: a flexible schedule, and access to numerous discounts. You're not locked into fixed vacation times, dictated by career responsibilities or children's school breaks. Taking the time to thoroughly investigate your options can save you a bundle. And it can also give you a feeling of being in control of your life, even if money's no object. The 89-year-old, retired steel company owner had no need to save money when he flew from Chicago to New York; if he did, he wouldn't have booked a suite at the Sherry Netherland for a week. But we all find pleasure in saving a little here and there. He flew on a now defunct "no-frills" airline, People Express, and got a big kick out of flying with the backpackers and youngsters who look for travel bargains to get where they're going.

Plan your travel carefully. Take advantage of your flexible schedule to keep transportation and accommodation costs to a minimum. There's no shame in finding the lowest possible rates, or asking questions about arrangements to make sure you get what you want. Here, time is money in your pocket, if you take the time to be a smart travel negotiator. Keep effective cost controls in place so you can stretch your travel budget to the maximum.

The travel industry recognizes the gold mine mature travelers represent, and is doing all it can to court them. Travel discounts based on age are no longer for senior citizens only. Membership in the American Association of Retired Persons, which you can join at 50, entitles you to discounts. There are also discount travel clubs open to anyone, that offer substantial discounts for people who can get up and go at the drop of a hat. If a conventional tour operator can't sell out an excursion, these clubs act as brokers, and with your open schedule, you're a prime candidate for taking advantage of this cut-rate travel.

Senior travel arrangements aren't only a matter of price. Package tours for seniors are put together because mature travelers expect a certain level of service and comfort; they don't have to rush through a tour like people who schedule nine countries in two weeks. Often, only travelers in upper-income brackets, that few younger travelers are in, can afford these trips anyway. Be aware of the full range of travel opportunities and possibilities now open to you.

When you do travel, don't assume getting a senior discount means that you've found the lowest fare or rate available. A savvy former financial planner with a reputation for cost cutting got a 15% senior discount at a hotel where he and his wife spent the weekend. When checking out he realized he could have gotten the same room at a 50% discount if he'd asked for the weekend package rate. Too late. Make sure you find the lowest rate available to anyone; that's not always the senior rate.

If possible, try to stage holiday gatherings at your headquarters, since travel is most expensive during peak holiday times. Visit out-of-town relatives when lower-cost, off-season travel is available.

You can negotiate some travel deals directly. If you're looking for accommodations in another city, call hotels directly and bypass the chain's toll-free 800 number. The individual hotels have more up-to-date information on their own room availability; if they need the business, you may be able to cut a deal with them that's better than any advertised discount.

Are You Too Obsessive about Your Interests?

An interviewer asked Pablo Casals, aged 90, if he ever practiced the cello anymore.

"Everyday!" Casals exclaimed.

"At your age you practice everyday?" asked the interviewer. "Why?"

"Because," Casals answered, "I think I'm getting better."

A former executive who was a prime candidate for cardiac arrest now walks around in designer sweats, quotes his split time in his last marathon, and watches every mouthful he eats lest it cut down on his speed. The knickknacks another started turning out in his toolroom workshop have turned into outdoor sculptures that have taken over the backyard. And still another spends hours in front of his personal computer, tracking his investments, and playing "what if" with an electronic spreadsheet. Is this behavior obsessive? No.

Enjoy yourself. If it isn't harmful or doesn't disrupt an important relationship, do what you want! If you've found something you like doing, and you find it totally consumes you, you've achieved post-career success. Don't worry about what the neighbors think, or view your life through the imagined eyes of former colleagues. You'll find the satisfaction that comes from working on something you enjoy and your control can be more psychically rewarding than a career. This stronger positive feedback leads some people to worry about going overboard with their enthusiasm. After all, they never got so excited about projects they worked on in their careers, and that's what everyone always told them was the most important part of life. If this is your "problem," consider yourself fortunate.

What If I Want to Do Nothing?

Some executives will have little trouble adapting to a life of simple leisure as described by the Mom and Pop Operation. Fine. There's nothing wrong with lying in a hammock if that's what you want to do. But here your semantics can send powerful, subconscious messages to yourself. Those who refer to a relaxed lifestyle as "doing nothing" are making a negative statement about themselves. It's impossible to be alive and not be doing something. When you say you're doing nothing, you're making a value judgment about how you spend your time; you're unproductive, wasting time. Your lifestyle is unsatisfying.

The definition of "doing nothing" is highly subjective. For the hard-driving Reactive or Overachiever, anytime not spent working, in the sense of a career, both before retirement and after, might be considered doing nothing. For others, spending a day at home because the rain is keeping you off the links is doing nothing. In general, we use the term to refer to time spent not pursuing our goals. If your goal is to relax, take it easy, and lead an unstructured life, and you're achieving that goal, you're not doing nothing. Enjoy it to the hilt, without guilt. Don't judge yourself by someone else's standards, and so explain to friends who are pursuing second careers or more active schedules that you're doing nothing. Otherwise you'll send the message to yourself and others that your life is unfulfilling. Soon, you'll start believing it.

Post-career Finances

Money management is an important part of everybody's post-career responsibilities. You don't have to pay attention to the Brussels stock exchange or run your financial projections through a computer to keep on top of your finances. All it takes is some simple and basic accounting procedures. Know how much is coming in and how much is going out. There are some basics of personal financial management:

- Have a budget, and stick to it.
- Maintain a list of all stocks and securities you own, and where they are.
- Examine your insurance annually, and change your coverage as your needs change.
- Maintain a list of all accounts, and records of your transactions.

Periodically review your situation with your financial advisory team. Do this either when you prepare your tax returns, or if you anticipate major expenditures or changing needs.

The Family

Without a career, we become much more emotionally dependent on family members. It's good and healthy to establish closer ties and more intimacy with those close to you, but don't let this backfire through unrealistic expectations and demands, either from you or on you.

Don't expect your idea of an evolving relationship shaped by retirement to be shared by others. Don't relocate to be near children or other close relatives unless you've discussed your plans with them. Your idea of an "occasional" get-together may be much more frequent than their idea. If you have married children, avoid battling over who they're going to spend the holidays with. At the same time, don't allow yourself to become the designated gofer under the assumption you've got nothing better to do. Keep the channels of communication open, but don't become ponderous, nagging or cranky in the guise of being open and honest. Retain your sense of humor.

GRANDPARENTING

Grandparenting can be an important component of post-career familial life. People seem to get a bigger kick out of being grandparents than they ever got out of being parents in the first place. As the grandchild sees it, it's the "good cop, bad cop" routine. The parents have to do the disciplining and put up with the tantrums. The grandparents get to be the ones who do the pampering. The relationship is extremely healthy for both grandparent and grandchild. A study of grandparent-grandchild interactions found grandchildren often provide, for mature individuals, the greatest sense of being "needed." The relationship is important for the emotional growth of the grandchild as well. No matter what one has done or achieved, few accomplishments equal the joy of having created a cohesive family. Don't deny yourself the opportunity to enjoy it.

YOUR PARENTS

Take your parents into account when planning for the future. Today's maturing executive is likely to have parents who may eventually need financial assistance and emotional support. Some of these executives belong to what's called the "sandwich generation"—they're providing support to both children and parents. The small research in this area indicates more than 10% of the executive population provides financial support to a parent or child, and that estimate could be low. Consider your parents' possible needs, and be prepared to deal with them. You may want to have a frank talk with them about plans for the future, and with their physicians to find out about any imminent health problems and overall vitality. Parents can resent and fear this intervention, but it's a subject that has to be addressed.

If you have siblings, arrange a discussion of your parents with them. Get a sense of what each is prepared to do to help. Don't make any assumptions about who's going to do what. While ideally the financial and emotional support should be shared equally, it's not always possible. You may be in a much better position to offer financial help. Another sibling may be unwilling to provide the emotional support, though quick with the wallet. Anticipate the needs of your parents in advance, and prepare for them to be met.

This helps you come to grips with your own aging as well as your parents', and will set the proper example for your children, too.

Quick-buck Artists, Scams and Scoundrels

People are bombarded by warnings about villainous types who prey on the unsuspecting retiree. Often we conjure up the image of a poor couple who bought a lot in the middle of the desert, hoping to retire there in spite of never having seen their dusty patch. But the better off you are, the bigger the target, and you'd be surprised at the number of sophisticated former executives who fall prey to fast talk and smooth con men. Former executives are particularly vulnerable, because:

- Their resources make them particularly attractive targets.
- They are anxious to be involved in something exciting and daring.
- They want to show they can still make money.

Why doesn't anybody believe the saying, "If it sounds too good to be true, it is," at the very moment they need to most?

Every day, thousands of con artists sit in offices and roam the roads of America, looking for opportunities at your expense. One showed up at the home of an ex-chemical engineer in Maryland, talking about the big profits in tomatoes. Right in your own backyard. The numbers showed it made sense. And the brochure certainly was impressive. The sincere salesman walked out with a $9,500 check for a complete greenhouse and tomato starter kit. It took a lot of work, and everybody in the family hated having to tend the tomatoes every day, watering and debugging them, but sure enough, they were growing big and beautiful just like the salesman said they would. Unfortunately, there was no place to sell them.

Being "taken" in retirement can be devastating, both emotionally and financially. One feels incredibly stupid and naive. It can create feelings indistinguishable from clinical depression, particularly when coupled with a sizable financial loss these incidents often represent. There are few parallels in the business world. The checks and balances of business generally minimize fraud and deceit of this kind. And unlike the business world, you can't come back tomorrow and make it up on the next deal. One more time with feeling: If it sounds too good to be true, it is!

Reviewing Your Business Plan

Reevaluate your business plan when goals or outside circumstances change, or whenever you feel there are problems with your current lifestyle. Among the changes that signal the need for reevaluation are:

- Major change in financial situation
- Significant dissatisfaction with current lifestyle
- Personal health crisis (physical, mental)
- Death or serious illness of spouse
- Relocation
- Employment status

Go through the inventories. Don't be afraid to rethink your situation. Have your interests changed? Are your objectives the same? What about new hobbies you want to pursue? Designating these as priority activities can give a boost to development efforts in new areas. Keep your log book where it's easy to get to. On a desk is better than in a drawer. Record thoughts and feelings that can signal changing priorities, new opportunities or problems. Take the thoughts you recorded into account during reevaluation.

Changing your plans isn't a sign of failure, or that you're doing something wrong. It's a sign that you're growing, and still prepared to meet the challenges of the future. You'll find, as in the business world, change is constant. What worked yesterday won't necessarily work tomorrow. Clinical evidence indicates people become *more* diverse and exhibit *more* individuality as they grow older. Like stars in an expanding universe, we continue to move apart from the status quo at an ever-accelerating rate. Be ready to keep moving! You'll need more room for your personality to grow in retirement than it needed in your career. Reevaluating your business plan helps you chart a course and track your growth and change.

As your post-career life progresses, prepare to make adjustments for the changes wrought by aging. There will be some slowing down of reflexes, some curtailment of physical activities. These changes aren't nearly as problematic as is people's lack of planning for them. Think about the adaptations that may be necessary in your home. You may want to move things from high shelves to make them easier to get to, or buy stronger lamps for reading. Don't look at these alterations as signs of decline. They're an indication you intend to remain in control of your life, and are taking steps to ensure it. One executive responded to decreased mobility by having a jacuzzi installed on the sundeck of his home. The hot circulating water helped keep his muscles limber, but it also made him feel "with it" to have the latest in youth-oriented leisure devices in full view.

Continue to challenge yourself, and keep your sense of humor and excitement about life. Put your lifetime of skills and resources to work, and you can manage to make retirement the most enjoyable career you've ever had.

APPENDIX A

COMPANY
RETIREMENT
PROGRAMS

"Executives are the most difficult group to get into preretirement counseling sessions."

—Neil Redford, Executive Vice President, Drake Beam Morin

If you're doing your planning properly, you know the kind of retirement training program your company offers. But you can't rely on company programs alone to solve your planning problems, no matter how thorough they are. In general, most suffer from four problems:

- They're not comprehensive enough.
- Emotional problems are downplayed.
- They're not aimed at all who need them.
- They take place late in the career.

Not Comprehensive Enough

Companies rarely devote the time and effort necessary to develop comprehensive retirement programs for executives. Even the most progressive companies are concerned first with the company's future, not the employees'. There's also a concern that aggressive retirement training programs will be perceived by employees as attempts to push them out the door, or as a form of subtle coercion.

Sometimes companies' best efforts at retirement training are undermined by the prospective retirees themselves. One company had to scale back an ambitious program after many attendees complained it was too involved. In order to keep employees participating, the company had to make the retirement training workshop more simplistic.

Emotional Complications Are Downplayed

Corporate programs focus on the "meat and potatoes" issues—how to manage retirement income, computing benefits, and health maintenance. While these areas are certainly important, emotional management is given short shrift. The result: Emotional problems are left to fester in the dark, and managers have no way of knowing the fallout is both natural and controllable.

They're Not Open to All Who Need Them

Since they focus on financial management, it's often assumed that the higher up on the corporate ladder, the less you need this kind of training. A senior executive is unlikely to have trouble making ends meet. Why should he come to a retirement seminar that's designed primarily to address this subject? One Fortune 500 company's retirement training program isn't even open to their top 100 executives. "These are superior people," the human resources director says. "They're extremely intelligent, and financially they have no problems whatsoever. They don't need our help."

If only that were true! In dealing with the emotional trauma retirement can bring, the higher up you go on the corporate ladder, the more you need effective transition help, and the less you get it. While lower-level execs also need to consider emotional management, the deck is stacked against the top executive when it's assumed intelligence and financial comfort protect him from post-career adjustment problems. It also sends the subliminal message that successful executives don't need to worry about retirement training or management. Whether they need help with financial planning or not, these are the people who may most feel the lack of the challenges, perks and non-cash benefits of their careers, and who have no place to turn to in order to get help with this transition.

Programs Start Too Late

If you don't start planning until the company puts the issue in front of you, you're behind schedule. Only the most progressive companies have programs that commence before executives reach the age of 55. That doesn't give enough time for the thorough planning you need. They can uncover looming post-career problems, but they often don't provide enough time to do anything about them.

A secondary problem is that many of these programs are "one time only." An executive who decides to get the jump on the situation by enrolling in a company program as early as possible may be enjoined from repeating it closer to retirement, should he wish to brush up on retirement planning issues.

If your company sponsors a retirement training program, by all means attend, and get as much as possible out of the experience. But be it a one-evening overview, or an intensive and ongoing program that involves you and your spouse, you can't expect them to take over the responsibility for proper planning from the one to whom it rightfully belongs—you! Nor can you expect them to devote the time to this all-important project that you can. Look upon company programs as a supplement to your own efforts and you'll be way ahead of the game—by being better prepared, and by exercising the initiative and self-reliance that is going to become more important than ever in your future.

The Basics of a Good Retirement Training Program

Compare your company's retirement training program with the elements of an ideal program, as listed below. Be ready to design your own retirement training program, incorporating these elements.

A good retirement training program:

• Commences well before retirement.

- Fully explains career/employment options.
- Provides financial planning help.
- Is ongoing and comprehensive.
- Deals with emotional issues.
- Encourages family participation.
- Includes one-on-one counseling.
- Takes into account an executive's position.
- Provides opportunities for "practicing" retirement.

Commences well before retirement. A good program starts while there's still time to do something about problem areas it uncovers. The earlier the better. Within five years of retirement is too late. Companies are steadily lowering the age at which executives are encouraged to participate, with progressive programs now commencing at age 50, or five years before an employee will first become eligible for retirement.

Fully explains career/employment options. A program should thoroughly cover the various avenues open to the executive, from early retirement to employment past traditional retirement age. Second careers, part-time work, and the facts about starting one's own business should be included. The program should clearly spell out the financial consequences of these options.

Provides financial planning help. Most key executives have access to financial planning assistance during their careers. Indeed, escalating salaries and intense competition for capable managers makes financial planning a valuable recruiting tool and executive perk. This help should also be available for retirement financial consultation, and indeed, it's the "hard" financial issues that get most of the attention in typical retirement training programs. Insurance, Social Security and Medicare benefits should be addressed.

Is ongoing and comprehensive. A weekend seminar or a group conference taking two weeknights isn't sufficient to deal with all the important retirement issues, including health maintenance, housing questions and development of activities.

Deals with emotional issues. Too many retirement programs ignore the psychological component of the retirement transition, with disastrous results. Executives can be left feeling there's something wrong with them if they don't smoothly glide into retirement. After all, if it was normal to have these kinds of problems, the training program would talk about it, right?

Encourages family participation. Wife, husband, lover, cat: If someone close will be sharing your future with you, he or she should be given the opportunity to assist in planning for it, and in having their desires taken into account. Including them in a retirement training program is an excellent way to solicit their input. (For more about spousal and family participation, see Chapter 9, "The Retirement Transition at Home.")

Includes one-on-one counseling. Group meetings are fine for bringing home the fact you're not the only one in the boat, but there are many issues maturing executives don't feel comfortable discussing in public. One-on-one discussions with a trained counselor give them an opportunity to talk about personal matters, or address harmless questions they simply don't want to raise in a group situation.

Takes into account an executive's position. In an effort to be thoroughly democratic, some major companies offer "one size fits all" programs—the janitor and the president have access to the exact same retirement training. This is a big mistake. The options, opportunities and problems they face are completely different, and therefore so should the preparatory work be.

Provide opportunities for "practicing" retirement. Good programs include a mechanism to let executives experiment with a retirement lifestyle, either through reduced responsibilities and/or reduced number of hours worked, or an unpaid leave to see what life after career is all about.

APPENDIX B

BENEFIT
PLANNING

Pensions, profit sharing and other benefit plans are complex and loaded with fine print. Knowing the intricacies of your benefits package can, in some cases, make the difference between establishing post-career financial security, and a future of scraping along. It's an area that demands your ongoing attention. New pension laws and rules are passed annually, as Congress tinkers with the Employee Retirement Income Security Act (ERISA), the legislation aimed at making sure pension plans are adequately funded.

Just as important as knowing what you've got coming to you is knowing how to choose from among the various methods of payout you're eligible for. Which payout you choose is a practical, highly individual decision, based on matters such as health, marital status, other income, and tax considerations. Once the payout decision has been made, it's usually irrevocable, so it's essential to have a full understanding of the options open to you, and the implications of each.

Assistance in selecting a pension payment option is one kind of help you shouldn't expect from company pension planners. Company officials are legally prohibited from giving financial advice to employees. This protects you from getting advice that benefits the company rather than you, and it protects the company from getting sued by employees who claim they were led astray in selecting a benefits package. (Some companies provide seminars on pension options conducted by independent licensed financial planners as part of their retirement counseling.) For this kind of advice, many executives consult their accountants, but few accountants are knowledgeable enough about pension disbursement for you to rely solely on their expertise. Plan to consult experts on income and estate planning, pension planning, and investments to decide how to hatch your pension nest egg.

Discussing your pension is an excellent way of getting you and your spouse to address the future jointly. In fact, in some cases it's a legal mandate. Some forms of pension payments can't be chosen without spousal approval.

In larger companies, managers may participate in several pension plans, such as stock accumulation, profit sharing, and defined benefits, all with various management objectives in mind. Some are aimed at binding executives to a company for the long haul, others for rewarding achievement of short-term economic goals. An executive may not have much ability to influence these pension plans, but their variety and the professional money management that guides them usually assures adequate capital appreciation.

Smaller companies, on the other hand, typically have less variety in plans, but this can be offset by the ability of executives to have a larger say in pension plan strategy and disbursement. An executive in a company like this needs to sit down with whoever is handling the pension plan—as far in advance as possible—and find out what latitude there is for designing a disbursement program that's most advantageous to the retiree.

It's also important to know what you won't get in a pension. Insurance and health benefits used to play a larger part in pension plans, but these benefits are slowly being reduced. A recent survey found 80% of the companies provide medical coverage for retirees, but pension planners expect this coverage to become a thing of the past. Medical benefits aren't a part of qualified plans, and with skyrocketing premiums for extended coverage, executives may have to pick up the tab for a policy that will augment their Medicare coverage.

This is very important, since Medicare is inadequate to cover your potential medical needs due to limits on per-illness costs on length of hospitalization beyond which medical benefits aren't payable.

Pensions don't have cost-of-living increases built in, either. Companies have no more idea about what will happen to the rate of inflation than anybody else, and won't make a promise to help retirees with rising prices, since steep inflation could wipe out pension reserves if cost-of-living increases were built in. During recent high inflationary periods some companies made adjustments to boost pension benefits voluntarily, but it's not something a retiree can depend on.

As you start to investigate, you'll encounter many or all of the following terms:

Defined Benefits Plan
Defined Contribution Plan
Vesting
Qualified Plan
Nonqualified Plan
Subsidized Benefits
Non-subsidized Benefits
Annuity
Life Annuity
Joint and Survivor Options
Year Certain
Payment Certain
Lump Sum Distribution

Defined Benefit Plan. This is a promise to pay a specific amount of benefits annually. The amount is usually pegged to a percentage of your final pay. For example, the defined benefit may be 75% of the average pay you received during your last three to five years of service. Often, the percentage is derived by multiplying a fixed number (like 1.5 or 2) times the number of years with the company. With a defined benefit plan, it's the responsibility of the employer to invest the pension funds wisely so that there's a sufficient amount to pay the defined benefit. Almost all defined benefit plans are guaranteed by the Federal Pension Benefit Guaranty Corp. up to approximately $20,000 per year, so even in the event of pension fund mismanagement, retirees have some protection.

Defined Contribution Plan. Here, a specific amount is contributed to the pension plan each year, typically a percentage of your compensation. These plans include profit sharing, money purchase pension plans, and stock bonus plans. Every participant has an account balance, and the way the money is invested has a direct bearing on what your benefits will be in retirement. Some plans let participants control the plan's investment direction, though this is rare; participant direction makes administrative costs soar. Semi-self-directed plans are more common. There may be a choice of several investment plans, giving participants a limited voice in how their money is invested.

Vesting. Vesting is the process by which pension contributions the company makes in your name become yours. Under the new tax law, companies can choose one of two vesting schedules to cover all employees: Either 100% vesting after five years of employment, or a graded vesting schedule. The graded schedule increases 20% annually beginning in the third year of employment, and reaches 100% vesting in the seventh year.

Under the five year, 100% vesting schedule, an employee who left in the fourth year of employment wouldn't get any company contributions made in his name, while if he waited six years he'd receive 100% of them. With the graded vesting schedule, the same employee would be entitled to 40% of his contributions after four years, and 80% after six. Under the new tax law, these schedules will take effect January 1, 1989.

Qualified Plan. The Internal Revenue Service Code establishes quidelines for setting up pension plans that allow employers to deduct contributions, and participants to escape taxes on benefits until they're paid out. If a plan meets these guidelines, it is said to be qualified. All the income generated is sheltered and the money is protected from creditors. Companies aren't required to have qualified pension plans, but since this is the only way to get tax breaks for establishing a pension plan, most are qualified.

Nonqualified Plan. Under the schedule of present laws, $90,000 is the maximum annual retirement benefit a company can bestow on an executive under a qualified plan. The maximum allowable benefit is reduced if the executive retires before the age of 65. What happens if you're making $350,000 annually, and your pension plan says you get 100% of your last year's pay? For these situations, companies have nonqualified deferred compensation plans.

Nonqualified plans don't have the extensive tax breaks for employers and participants accorded qualified plans. While there may be tax advantages in exercising some stock options that are often a part of nonqualified deferred compensation, these plans are usually nothing more than a promise to pay. If assets or funds are set aside for this purpose, they're subject to "substantial risk of forfeiture"—that means they can be taxed, attached by creditors, or be used up for other purposes if the need suddenly arises. If you're promised benefits from a nonqualified plan, it's a good idea to ascertain the measures the company is taking to fund its obligations. You should also pay attention to the overall fortunes of the company, and avoid having too much deferred compensation tied up in a nonqualified plan.

Subsidized and Non-subsidized Plans. Many plans have built-in early retirement provisions, allowing executives to begin collecting a pension as soon as they accumulate a certain number of years of service, or a number that represents a combination of their age and years of service. For example, you may be eligible for a pension if your age and years of service add up to 70. If the pension is non-subsidized, your payments would be reduced to reflect the longer period for which you'd be expected to collect your pension; it is "actuarially equivalent" to the payments you'd receive if you didn't retire early. On the other hand, a subsidized plan gives early retirees somewhat more than an actuarially equivalent one, and the average beneficiary will receive more pension benefits over his lifetime. Subsidized plans are typically found in pensions of companies that want to encourage early retirement. However, companies with subsidized plans can overcome this built-in early retirement inducement by offering higher pay and bonuses to valuable senior executives.

Annuity. An annuity is simply a series of payments. A pension is an annuity, guaranteeing a series of payments during retirement. It may be paid by an employer, administered for your employer by an insurance company, or paid as life insurance. There are several common options in selecting a pension annuity. Qualified pension plans must meet legal requirements for providing income for a secondary beneficiary, such as a spouse, after the retiree's death.

The option selected determines the amount of money in each payment, and the length of time the payments continue. Actuarially speaking, the longer your annuity is calculated to continue being paid, the less money in each individual payment. It's essential to give careful consideration to what kind of pension annuity to select. In most cases the selection is irrevocable.

Single Life/Straight Life Annuity. A life annuity provides a monthly pension payment for the life of the retiree. However, once the retiree dies, no payments will be made to his survivor. Pensions are now considered community property, so a married retiree must have his spouse's written permission to receive a life annuity. This protects spouses' pension rights, but it can also cause problems for prospective retirees who have been separated from their spouses for long periods of time.

Joint and Survivor Options. These are life annuities that cover two people. Most married executives choose this kind of retirement compensation. While it reduces the amount the retiring executive (the primary beneficiary) receives monthly, it ensures that the spouse will continue getting checks even after the death of the primary beneficiary. If the spouse dies before the primary beneficiary a new survivor beneficiary can't be named.

The amount the primary beneficiary's survivor receives varies with the kind of option chosen. For example, a joint and 50% survivor annuity means that following the death of the primary beneficiary, the survivor would get half of the amount received while the primary beneficiary was alive. There would be no reduction if a joint and 100% option were chosen, but the amount of these payments during the primary beneficiary's life would be smaller to begin with. Under some joint and survivor annuity plans, payments are reduced upon the death of either beneficiary.

Year Certain/Term Certain. Here the primary beneficiary receives penison payments for life, while providing continued benefits to a secondary beneficiary only within a finite period of time. For example, with a ten-year certain plan, if the primary beneficiary dies within ten years of the first pension payment, the secondary beneficiary will receive benefits until ten years from that first payment. If an executive with this year certain coverage dies after nine years, his survivor receives benefits for another one year.

If the primary beneficiary dies after ten years, his survivor receives no further payments.

Generally, this kind of arrangement can make sense if the primary or secondary beneficiary expects to come into a large sum of money at a specific date in the future, or if the secondary beneficiary is in poor health and not expected to survive very long.

Payment Certain. As money is contributed to your pension plan, you build up a "pension reserve." This is an amount of money set aside at retirement to ensure there'll be enough money to continue pension payments for the rest of your life. With "payment certain," you're guaranteed to receive at least the amount in your pension reserve. Should you die before receiving benefits that equal the reserve, your beneficiary will receive the remainder. Should you live long enough so that your pension payments exceed the pension reserve, you'll still get pension income, but a beneficiary would receive no benefits after your death. Generally, the retiree can designate a new beneficiary under the payment certain option.

Lump-sum Distribution. This is the "take the money and run" theory of post-career financial management. You're given a fat paycheck as a one-time benefit payment and you're on your own.

Many companies are ending lump-sum distribution options. In smaller companies, if enough people take a lump-sum distribution, it can affect the pension's investment position, and jeopardize the whole plan. Larger companies discourage lump-sum payments for other reasons. Employers haven't always been consistent with how they compute the lump sum, and there's been lots of litigation brought by disgruntled retirees who feel they got less than someone else. Some companies stipulate only retirees who can prove a certain net worth, or who can produce a certified statement from an accountant vouching for the wisdom of the lump-sum payment decisions, are eligible for it. Other companies make those who want the big payback prove they're in good health. Why? Because of what insurance companies call "adverse selection." If you're in great health you might choose an annuity if it were on good rates because you have reasonably good expectations of sticking around long enough to milk it for all it's worth. Those in bad health, the reasoning goes, wouldn't receive much from an annuity if they die soon after retirement. Therefore, they take the lump-sum payment.

Those interested in lump sum distributions must thoroughly investigate the tax ramifications. Unless the payment is effectively sheltered, such as by a rollover into an IRA or five-year forward averaging, a large chunk can wind up in Uncle Sam's pocket.

BIBLIOGRAPHY

American Association of Retired Persons. *Looking Ahead—How to Plan Your Successful Retirement.* Washington, D.C.: American Association of Retired Persons, 1985.

Anastasi, Anne. *Psychological Testing*, 4th edition. New York: Macmillan, 1976.

Bonoma, Thomas V. and Dennis P. Slevin. *Executive Survival Manual.* Boston: CBI, 1978.

Bradford, Leland P. and Martha I. *Retirement: Coping with Management Upheavals.* Chicago: Nelson-Hall, 1976.

Bright, Deborah. *Gearing Up for the Fast Lane.* New York: Random House, 1985.

Buckley, Joseph C. *The Retirement Handbook*, revised edition. New York: Harper and Brothers, 1962.

Butler, Robert N., M.D., and Herbert P. Gleason, editors. *Productive Aging.* New York: Springer, 1985.

Chapman, Elwood N. *Comfort Zones.* Los Altos, California: Crisp Publications, 1985.

Charlesworth, Edwin A., Ph.D., and Ronald G. Nathan, Ph.D. *Stress Management.* New York: Ballantine, 1985.

Columbia University College of Physicians and Surgeons. *Complete Home Medical Guide.* New York: Crown, 1985.

Downes, John and Jordan Elliot Goodman. *Barron's Finance and Investment Handbook.* Woodbury, New York: Barron's, 1986.

Ehrenberg, Miriam, Ph.D., and Otto Ehrenberg, Ph.D. *Optimum Brain Power.* New York: Dodd, Mead, 1985.

Flach, Frederick F., M.D. *Choices.* Philadelphia: J.B. Lippincott, 1977.

Friedman, Lawrence M. *Your Time Will Come: The Law of Age Discrimination and Mandatory Retirement.* New York: Russell Sage Foundation, 1985.

Goldsmith, Sharon, R.N. *Human Sexuality.* St. Louis: C.V. Mosby, 1986.

Goleman, Daniel. *Vital Lies, Simple Truths.* New York: Simon and Schuster, 1985.

Jaffe, Dennis T. and Cynthia D. Scott. *From Burnout to Balance.* New York: McGraw-Hill, 1984.

Jud, Robert, *The Retirement Decision.* New York: Amacom, 1981.

Lesko, Matthew. *Information U.S.A.* New York: Penguin, 1983.

Maas, Henry S., and Joseph A. Kuypers. *From Thirty to Seventy.* San Francisco: Jossey-Bass, 1974.

Michaels, Joseph. *Prime of Your Life.* New York: Facts On File, 1983.

Miller, Sigmund Stephen, Julian Asher Miller, and Don Ethan Miller. *Lifespan Plus.* New York: Macmillan, 1986.

Montana, Patrick J. and Margret V. Higginson. *Career Life Planning for Americans.* New York: Amacom, 1978.

Morris, Charles G. *Psychology,* 2nd edition. Englewood Cliffs, New Jersey: Prentice-Hall, 1976.

Nolen, William A., M.D. *Crisis Time!* New York: Dodd, Mead, 1984.

Posner, Mitchell J. *Executive Essentials.* New York: Avon, 1982.

Potter, Beverly A., Ph.D. *The Way of the Ronin.* New York: Amacom, 1984.

Schuman, Nancy, and William Lewis. *Back to Work.* Woodbury, New York: Barron's, 1985.

Sibson & Company. *Executive Compensation Annual Report 1986.* New York: Sibson & Company, 1986.

Stillman, Richard J. *Guide to Personal Finance*, 4th edition. Englewood Cliffs, New Jersey: Prentice-Hall, 1984.

Tane, Lance D. "Guide to Successful Flex Plans: Four Companies' Experiences," *Compensation and Benefits Review* (July-August 1985).

Vicker, Ray. *Retirement Planning.* Homewood, Illinois: Dow Jones-Irwin, 1985.

Wilcock, Keith D. *The Corporate Tribe.* New York: Warner Books, 1984.

The Wyatt Company. *Top Fifty—A Survey of Retirement, Thrift and Profit-sharing Plans Covering Salaried Employees of 50 Large U.S. Industrial Companies. As of January 1, 1985.* New York: The Wyatt Company, 1985.

INDEX

Acceptance (stage), 7, 8-9, 11, 16, 98; in early retirement, 195; exercises, 110, 138-39; redefining yourself in, 109-10; and retirement transition at home, 121, 127-39; and retirement transition in office, 105-9
Activities, 41-42, 79
Activity development fund, 133, 163, 176
Activity development exercises, 132-33
Adaptation: administration, 58-59; analysis, 47-48; communication, 49-50; creativity, 45-46; flexibility, 56-57; implementation, 54; planning, 51-52
Adjustment, 221-26; to aging, 236
Administration (management skill), 43, 44, 58-60; personal project for, 61
Age Discrimination, 200-1
Agenda, 40, 51-52, 65, 92, 98; leisure activities, 132; personal, 110; post-career, 90, 216, 220
Aging, 6, 181, 234, 236; fear of, 12-13; inability to accept, 83; and nutrition, 178-79; physiological changes in, 161-62, 166, 182; and sexuality, 182; of spouse, 125
Alcohol use/abuse, 2, 21, 180-181
American Association of Retired Persons, 138, 221, 230
American Express, 164
American Heart Association, 156
American Management Association, 107
American Psychological Association, 153
Analysis (management skill), 43, 44, 47-48, 102-3; and early retirement, 194; personal project for, 60
Anger, 11, 13-14, 16
Announcements (retirement), 115-16, 144-45
Anxiety, 7, 12, 81, 210
Aspen Institute, 67
AT&T, 195, 226
Attitude(s), 84; and eating habits, 174-75; and health, 81-82, 153-

59; about money, 85; and stress, 154-55, 158-59, 162; about work, 186, 187

Benefit planning, 243-50
Benefits, 107, 109; in early retirement, 191, 201
Board of advisors, 29-30, 137, 159, 164
Boredom, 83, 144, 180
Bowen, John C., 2, 19-21
Budget, 58, 86, 146, 232; activity development fund in, 133, 163; educational, 223; travel, 229
Business, starting own, 88, 158
Business/employment possibilities: inventory of, 75, 83-84, 87, 133, 199
Business interests, 222
Business plan: reviewing, 235-36
Busy work, 41, 133

Calendar, planning, 143-44
Capitalization requirements, 85
Career, 83, 105; and family relationships, 76-77; fitness and, 162-64; post-career thoughts about, 217-19; retirement as, 39-40; termination of dependence on, 216
Career commitment, 5-6, 122; reduction of, 110, 111-13
Career dependence, 91, 216, 218
Career/employment options: in retirement training programs, 240
Career goals, 107, 201; vs. life goals, 100, 101-3
Career identification, 5, 6, 91-92, 218
Career relationship, 3, 4, 17; and retirement transition, 5-16
Career review, 105, 115
Career satisfaction, 5, 6
Carnegie-Mellon University, 67
Casals, Pablo, 230-31
Challenges, 42, 92, 120, 186, 187, 236
Change, 236; adaptation to, 56, 57; economic, 193; and stress, 12, 154-55; see also Corporate restructuring
Charity work, 71, 221
Children, 176, 233, 234;

254